GW00391755

PLUGS AND PLUG FISHING

Plugs and plug fishing

Barrie Rickards

and

Ken Whitehead

*with 66 photographs
and 20 diagrams*

Adam and Charles Black
London

First published 1976
A. & C. Black Ltd
London WC1R 4JH

© 1976 Barrie Rickards and Ken Whitehead

ISBN 0 7136 1620 2

All rights reserved.
No part of this publication may be
reproduced, stored in a retrieval system, or
transmitted, in any form or by any means,
electronic, mechanical, photocopying,
recording or otherwise, without the prior
permission of A. & C. Black Ltd.

Filmset by Keyspools Ltd, Golborne, Lancashire
Printed in Great Britain by
Butler and Tanner Ltd, Frome and London

Contents

Acknowledgements

We should like to thank *all* the anglers, tackle dealers and tackle firms who have offered advice and loaned equipment, but would particularly thank Eric Hodgson, Les Beacroft and Martin Gay, who have gone out of their way to help in many matters; Ken Latham of Potter Heigham to whom so many plug addicts owe such a lot; Messrs Woolco, Ken Morritt of Intrepids, and also Milbro Sports, who have a faith in us we hope to live up to. Thelma Norman sorted out much of our manuscript with her usual skill, and Tony Perrin of Abu gave a lot of help and forward thinking. Adrian Lawson and Alan Vare kept up a non-stop stream of arguments and criticism – and also posed patiently for us when we needed photographs. To all, we offer our grateful thanks.

Foreword

Probably most freshwater anglers come to plug fishing through pike fishing, and we were no exceptions. We remember buying those rather tatty blue, scale-finished, jointed wooden floaters. They had double hooks that were none too strong, and half a season's use was enough to remove the paint which cracked and scratched off just as easily as it does off pike floats. But those plugs worked well and, indeed, they are still on the market, though now not as popular as the well-finished plastic products available today. The first thing that struck us, all those years ago, was that a 4- to 5-inch jointed plug produced rather more big pike than little spinners which most anglers used. To this day neither of us has taken a twenty-pound pike on plug, but we've had a lot of big doubles, and very many pike of smaller sizes. It is a tremendous way of piking, and we have each spent more time in the past twenty years using plugs than any other bait. Obviously, we are not competent to instruct on how to catch giant pike on plugs, though this kind of success *has* come to a few anglers in recent years; this book is about how to catch, and enjoy catching, as many pike as possible; or as many perch; or as many chub. . . .

During the preparation of this work we became aware that nowhere was there a single concise pocket-book of information for the plug addict. It was easy enough to find a chapter on plug fishing in a general book on fishing, but what does the plug addict do if he wishes to ply his technique from a boat? Does he find another book on boat fishing? Archie Black was much in favour of getting between the covers as much information as would help the plug fisherman irrespective of the circumstances and, within the limits of our experience, irrespective of the quarry.

Therefore, we have begun with Part I on the plugs themselves – good ones, bad ones, how to make them and so on; then in Part II we have dealt with all the other tackle a plug fisherman needs, or needs to consider. The approach we have used has meant that some topics are buried in the text: thus we have a section on casting (Chapter 12), but playing and landing are contained in the sections on rods and miscellaneous tackle since it would have been repetitive to have separate sections on these subjects. Otherwise the section headings are, we hope, self-explanatory.

Part III deals with plug fishing for certain species since, notwithstanding what has been said previously, each species needs a special approach. For example, you need a wire trace for pike fishing; for zander their use is debatable; for perch and chub plugging they are unnecessary. Our experience is not broad enough to cover plug fishing for all species, but we give a pointer or two in the general direction of game fishing and sea angling. In the last sphere, plug fishing in this country has probably not yet taken the hold that it undoubtedly will, and most sea anglers are probably not much more experienced than ourselves in bashing out mackerel and pollack. But the time will come, as it has already with bass fishing.

Throughout the text we have tried to capture something of the atmosphere of plug fishing: there is a depth of enjoyment about it, for us, which is not quite there even when using spoons and spinners. Spoons and spinners are cold bits of metal, and there is no real pretence at imparting life into them. But in plugging you can creep a plug across the top of a weed bed and make it behave for all the world like a small, lone fish carefully reconnoitring its way through a jungle inhabited by big pike – and that's exactly what it *is* doing.

PART ONE
The plugs themselves

I

Introducing plugs

DEFINITION OF A PLUG

A plug is an artificial lure, usually made of wood or plastic, and most often designed to look something like a fish. We say 'something like' rather than 'resembling' because many plugs resemble almost nothing on earth – except in action in the water, where they may take on a vitality very attractive to the angler's prey. Plugs can be classified in various ways, and one classification hinges on the last character: some are built to resemble fish and their action is supposed to be close to that of either a healthy or an injured fish; others have little resemblance to a fish but have an action, usual vibrant, which alone attracts the attention of the predator.

They can also be classified by the manner in which they are retrieved through the water: some float or splash on the surface; others float when stationary but dive to various depths when retrieved; yet others sink at varying speeds and can be returned to the rod in a bewildering number of ways.

It should not be supposed that plugs are totally distinct from other artificial lures such as spinners and flies. They are not. In fact the three types are connected by a range of intermediates. Some 'spinners' have a fixed head, often made of rubber, situated just before a revolving blade. To British anglers the Voblex (Fig. A) will be the most familiar in this category, but there are many others. Abu, for example, make the Morrum-spinner in weights up to $\frac{5}{8}$ oz, whilst Bomber Baits of Gainesville, Texas, make a huge range of Gimmick 'spinner flies' which have variously-coloured heads including bulbous eyes, rotating blade, and feathered hooks (Fig. B). Again, many jigs are little more than simplified plugs with or without the addition of feathers: Bomber Baits make the Gumpy Jig (Fig. C) for example.

At one time definition of a plug was fairly easy if all that was required was distinction from spinners: if it had a revolving blade it was a spinner. Nowadays, however, nobody in his right mind would term Shakespeare's Slim Jim a spinner since it is patently a plug, but with tiny propeller-like blades at the head and tail. Probably it is best to call an artificial bait a fly (using the word in a broad sense to include the modern reservoir anglers' 'lures') if it contains a preponderance of feather over hard body; and an artificial bait a spinner if it is built with more obvious blades than hard body!

Having said all that it remains to mention, of all things, a creature called the Spoon-plug (Fig. D). This is made entirely of metal, but on retrieve behaves like a plug, with a very powerful and vibrant wobble and a tendency to dive very deeply. Indeed, the diving ability is so great that casting and retrieving from the bank is next to impossible, and the lure is best fished from a boat. It is extremely good for trolling and has accounted for some big lake trout. Although it is not readily available in this country, it should not be beyond the skill of many anglers to make their own, experimenting with different thicknesses of metal and different sizes of Spoon-plug.

It will be clear from the above that the great variation possible in basic design will lend itself to inventiveness on the part of the angler – one of the great joys of plug fishing – and this we hope to explain more fully in the chapter on home-made plugs. Later we shall also give a fuller account of the manner in which plugs work in the water.

AMERICAN IMPORTS

Many years ago when wielding a battered and scratched wooden plug at Eastrington in East Yorkshire, Barrie came across a group of rather well-to-do gentlemen who had, in addition to deer-stalkers, a few dozen glossy, posh, colourful (colorful) American plugs. Since they didn't do as well as Barrie that day he dismissed their plugs as useless and gawdy to boot. This attitude stayed with British anglers for many years, with a few stalwarts such as Bernard Venables insisting that American plugs could be good, but resistance was eventually broken down by a handful of enthusiasts who proved beyond

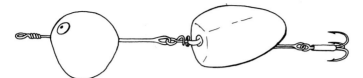

Fig. **A**

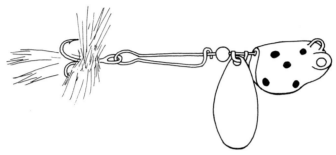

Fig. **B**

Fig. **C**

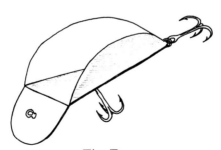

Fig. **D**

doubt that plugs from over the Atlantic were first-class. We are thinking, of course, of anglers like Ernest Merritt, Fred J. Taylor, Fred Wagstaffe, Mike Muse, and Bob Reynolds. Some British tackle shops, Ken Latham's of Potter Heigham for example, realised the value of these plugs and made a great effort to supply British anglers. Thanks to these anglers a variety of plugs is available in most medium to large towns in the country. Did we say 'a variety'? What we mean is terrific variety, with plugs to do things that grandfather would have thought impossible.

But if you take into consideration the plugs available in all the catalogues, Heddon, Shakespeare, Abu, Bomber etc. the variety is quite overwhelming. Or is it?

THE GREAT VARIETY OF PLUGS

Towards the beginning of the book (Chapter 2) we attempt, perhaps unwisely, to give a basic classification of plugs in relation to other lures. But what we want to talk about here is the variety even within that basic scheme. Lay out twenty catalogues on the floor and prepare to gasp! The colour, shape and size variation is staggering. But wait, things are not quite what they seem: most of the plugs *do* fall into our classification, but furthermore it soon becomes apparent that very, very similar plugs are made by different manufacturers.

Thus Bill Norman's Shiner-minnows are very similar to Normark Vibro's famous Rapalas, and both provide us with moderate divers with slim, elongate, scaly bodies. Abu and Whopper Stopper make similar plugs although these tend to work at slightly different depths for a similar retrieve.

Amongst the deep divers Bomber's Waterdog is not unlike Whopper Stopper's Hellbender. Both are available in a range of colours which are not, in fact, as similar as the bodies with their trailing tail-spoons. The Lazy Ike series of banana-shaped or 'flatfish' plugs have been made in very similar fashion by other firms.

And so it goes on: on the home front, Woolworth's sell several plugs which are at least comparable to the more expensive foreign designs. In other words, although things are at first sight bewildering to the beginner, all that the duplication from firm to firm achieves is to give the angler a wider choice of *colours* for his favourite design.

2

Classification of plugs

We have already given some hint of the difficulties here in the section defining what we mean by a plug: the spoon plugs, for example, high-light the problem. But the flow diagram (Fig. E) is a valiant attempt (we think) to draw up a basic classification of plugs, with examples, and at the same time show their relationships to other kinds of lures: spoons, spinners, flies and so on. No classification can be perfect, and an obvious drawback to ours is that the words FLIES, SPINNERS and SPOONS on the right of the diagram could be interchanged, since each can be used at any depth. On the other hand we prefer to retain the depth parameter for the rest of the diagram where it is readily applicable.

Let's have a look at the way plugs merge into spinners, spoons and flies: we'll begin at the surface and work down towards the depths. Some of the surface poppers such as Norman's Chuggerflash are surface plugs in the strictest sense, but others like small feathered poppers are little more than flies and are probably fished better *as* flies on fly rods and lines. In passing, we should mention that flies also merge into spinners as the blades get smaller and the amount of feather greater: the Abu-fly is a good example although there are several others.

Bomber's Gimmick and Bushwhacker range have a small plug-like head, particularly the former, but otherwise are more nearly like fly-spoons, that is, with a considerable amount of feather and attendant spoons as well! Such lures almost defy classification, but you can see that on our flow diagram they are situated at the SPINNER end of the BORDERLINE group of plugs. They are really plug-like spinners with fly affinities, hence we have drawn arrows indicating their connections.

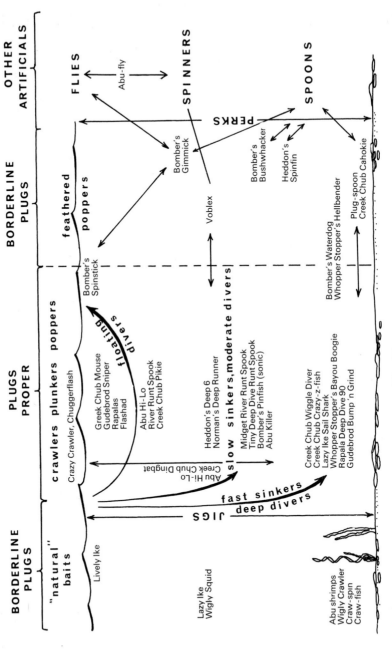

Fig. E

The same principle has been used with the placing of other lures of doubtful affinity. Thus Heddon's Spinfin has an almost plug-like body and associated spoon and hair: it is basically a deeper-fished spoon bait with plug affinities and we have it in the BORDERLINE group with arrows showing its relationships.

Going deeper than the Heddon's Spinfin we have Bomber's Waterdog, and Whopper Stopper's Hellbender. Both are plugs almost in the strict sense, with nearly horizontal diving vanes which take them on very deep dives, but they have small spoons appended at the tail end of the plug. Thus we place them, in our classification, deep in the water and with connections with both plugs and spoons.

A couple of lures which hold a similar position in terms of depth to the Waterdog and Hellbender are the Plug-spoon and Creek Chub Cahokie. These are all-metal and more spoon-like than plug-like and hence are at the spoon end of the BORDERLINE group. They work extremely deep and, unlike most plugs, are fast sinkers. Quite a few other lures are made which fall into the BORDERLINE group between plugs on the one hand and flies, spinners and spoons on the other, but it is not our intention to discuss them or their placings in detail. Indeed, it is useful for the user of our chart to try to place his own lures, look for exceptions, and then try to build up a better, perhaps three-dimensional classification.

There are two other relatively simple borderline types to consider in our groupings. Perks are *almost* spoons, *almost* spinners, and *almost* flies, depending on the type in use. They can be used at all depths, but particularly are deep-water lures. Jigs can be *almost* plugs in that they have a plug-like body even though they are often heavily adorned with feathers; they also merge into perks and flies! Jigs are operated at any depth, usually deep, and some, such as Rapala jigs, can be imparted with a very fish-like action by jerking them up and down with the rod end.

A few other borderline types are shown on the left of our diagram, and we hope their positions are more or less self-explanatory: they have a claim to represent 'natural' baits. The excellent Abu shrimps could be considered either as jigs or perks, whilst the bottom-crawlers like Heddon's Craw-spin and Lazy Ike's Craw-fish are probably closer to jigs than to anything else.

Returning now to the centre of our diagram, the 'plugs proper', we have tried to classify them in terms of the depths at which they work. Thus we have crawlers, plunkers and poppers at the surface; then floating shallow divers, followed by floating moderate divers coupled with slow sinkers; then floating deep divers and, finally, fast sinkers. Several things are apparent, such as the fact that the Abu Hi-Lo range and Creek Chub Dingbat transgress this classification because they have adjustable diving vanes and come into each of our depth categories.

Many other plugs *are* restricted, however, and one very obvious point is that whilst floating and shallow divers are made in abundance by many firms, fast sinkers, and even really deep divers, are far less common.

Amongst the fast sinkers the Lazy Ike Sail Shark, with its 'sonic vibration' is outstanding, whilst Whopper Stopper's Bayou Boogie can be sunk to any depth *and worked at that depth*. Creek Chub's Cray-z-fish and Wiggle Diver can be got down deeply and quickly, but having said that we have almost exhausted the readily available fast sinkers.

There are, of course, some good deep divers: Rapala Deep Dive 90; Gudebrod Bump 'n Grind. If these are used with the 'borderline' Waterdogs and Hellbenders the angler has a useful coverage with deep divers, although nothing like that which he has with floating shallow and moderate divers. We have heard many anglers say that in British waters they cannot catch much on the Gudebrod Bump 'n Grind: contrast that with the reputation of the Gudebrod Sniper, and it is certainly no accident that most of the famous plugs are essentially shallow or top-water types.

We cannot emphasize too strongly that our naming of the above plugs and lures is merely for the purpose of explaining our classification, although we have tended to use the plugs we have found successful. We do not intend to imply that many other plugs are not just as good, and we invite the reader to attempt to classify his own favourites on our scheme.

PLUG ACTION

So far we have talked about floating, diving, deep diving actions etc. The time now has come to sort out these in more detail to avoid confusion later on. When the manufacturer produces a plug he designs the model to work at, or rather between, certain sections of the water.

His idea in this is to imitate a particular fish, or fish action, and the mechanics of the plug will give the best results when they are used within the tolerance he describes.

This does not mean that the plug *cannot* be made to work in a different section of the water, but if it is used in any way other than that for which it was designed, the action will probably be impaired.

As an instance of this, think about a surface lure. It is designed to work on the surface only. You can fix lead on the trace above the line and cause it to sink – but if you do, its action and attraction, i.e. sputtering around with bags of noise and fuss, will be lost. There are plugs on the market that can be adjusted to work at several depths by adjustment of the plug fittings, or where the use of lead is recommended, but they are few and far between.

SURFACE LURES

These plugs always float on the surface, and are designed to remain there during the retrieve. They are made of wood, or plastic with in-built buoyancy. In shape they are usually pointed or with a 'pug'

I SURFACE LURES. I. Crazy Crawler   2. Sinner Spinner   3. Trouble Maker   4. Mr Thirteen.

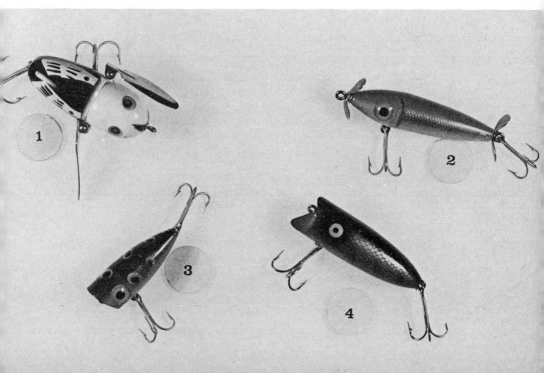

end sloping backwards, to give the plug lift as it is pulled through the water. Sometimes there are spinning blades at either end of the body, or metal vanes standing out from the head or body itself.

The idea with these is to cause water disturbance and strange though it may seem, this very noise (some of them kick up Hell's delight) is the very secret of their success.

They are designed to be retrieved slowly, or 'popped' back to the fisherman in small jerks that disturb the water – rather like an insect struggling on the surface. They fish best under trees, and around reed beds, fallen trees – places in fact where surface splashing creatures would be found.

FLOATING–DIVING LURES

When not being retrieved, the floating–diving lure rests on the surface of the water. Once a retrieve is started, or the rod top moved, then they will commence a shallow dive, the depth of dive being governed by the rate of retrieve itself. The dive effect is produced by

2 FLOATING DIVERS. 1. Big 'S' 2. Flashad 3. Sniper 4. Meadow Mouse 5. Wood Basser 6. Tiger 7. Mr Thirteen 8. Tadpole.

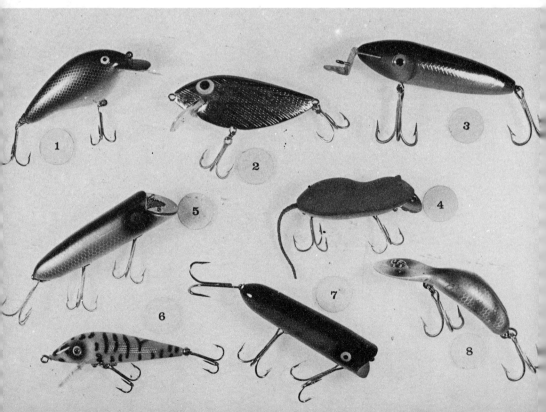

a vane, or lip of metal, or sometimes the shape of the nose at the head of the lure, which acts as a paravane.

With a little thought this type of plug can be made to perform just about every action in the fishing calendar, from a switchback up and down to the sideways lunge produced with rapid retrieve. Sensible use of the rod top, twitching and changing direction of the rod from one side of the angler's body to the other during the retrieve, all promote a tremendous amount of life.

SINKING PLUGS

These are for deep water and holes where weight is needed to get the plug down into the fishing layer. After the lure has hit the surface, count the lure down, perhaps counting three – then start the retrieve. Next cast count four, and so on. Once the taking depth of fish is found, keep to that count-down, and you will be in their approximate feeding depth. Most of the plugs in this category really look like fish, although a few do have a vane or lip to help keep them down. Often

3 SINKING PLUGS. 1. Commando 2. Snoky 3. Sonic 4. Mr Murder 5. Punkin Seed 6. Killer.

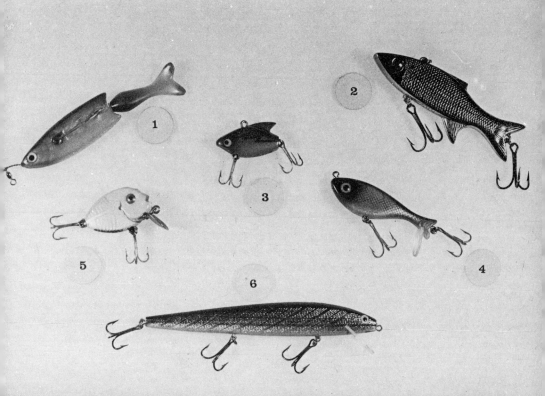

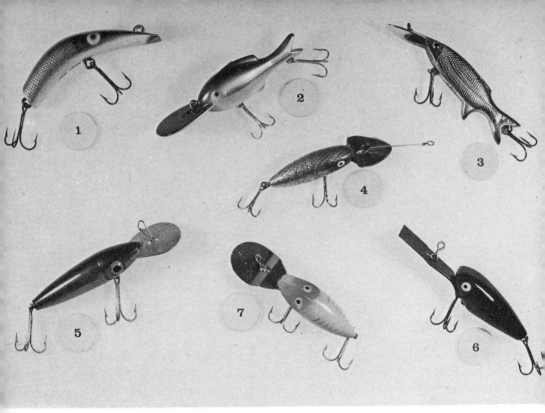

4 DEEP DIVING LURES.   1. Lazy Ike   2. Crackleback   3. Snoky   4. Cisco
Kid   5. Bump 'n Grind   6. Deep 6   7. Deep Dive River Runt Spook.

a fish will take on the drop. If the plug has an in-built vibrator – usually a metal ball inside a hollowed out section of the body – then the
manufacturers advise a speed-up in the retrieve to make the maximum effect.

DEEP DIVING PLUGS

These may have a floating or sinking body, but are recognised by the
long, wide metal lip that planes them down quickly once the retrieve
is started. If you are using a sinker, then use the count-down method
and start the action at varying depths until the fish are found. Naturally, these are the plugs to use when trolling.

Now that we have discussed a little of the varieties and classified
plugs by their action, we can follow with a description of a few favourites of ours, and what we like (or dislike) about each one. But they

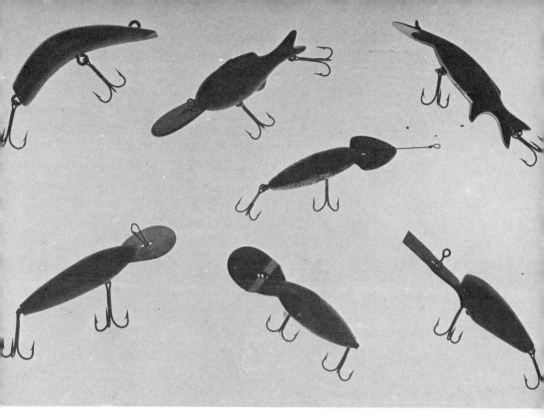

5 The same lures – deep divers – seen in silhouette, as a fish sees them.

are only a few from our box; to describe them all would fill another book.

3

Some good plugs

GUDEBROD SNIPER

We have used this plug in the 4-inch length on the fenland drains with great success. Under dull conditions the yellow version is good, and under bright conditions the duller perch-striped model succeeds well. On one occasion Barrie and Ray Webb were working slowly along a small fenland drain and although they had moved a pike or two all had come short of the usually successful spinner, a red-tagged Veltic No. 5. A change to the yellow Sniper by Barrie resulted in three pike in three casts; whereupon Ray switched to the perch-striped example, the only other one they had, and immediately began to take fish.

We have also done well on Loch Lomond with the same plugs, and the ideal situation for their use seems to be relatively shallow water, say 2- to 5-feet, with a thickish growth of weed in the lowest two-thirds with strands reaching to the surface. On a short cast of about twenty yards the plugs can be worked very slowly at depths down to two feet or so: each plug varies slightly in the depth at which it can be worked. A very slow retrieve produces an incredible wobble which pike and perch certainly find hard to resist, and they come out of the sunken weed-beds like bullets.

The plugs are heavy and cast well, but do have a number of defects. The treble hooks are simply attached to ring-headed screws, and these latter do pull out occasionally. Nor is the seal very good, for on each plug used we have suffered eventually from water getting inside the body. This causes the plug to sink and the action is killed anyway. The cure for these plugs, when waterlogged, is to drill a couple of fine holes in the body to let out the water, dry them, seal the holes with Araldite, and finally give the whole plug a coating or two of polyurethane varnish.

Just recently (1974) it has become difficult to obtain the 4-inch version of the Sniper, but we believe Watson's of Nottingham still have the $2\frac{7}{8}$-inch size in stock. It would be a great pity if this plug was lost to British anglers, although it would not be the first to be so.

NORMARK VIBRO RAPALA

Omri Thomas of Vibro let us have a set of these a few years ago. We have not yet lost a single one, and we dread doing so, for their scratched and tattered appearance bears witness to the savagery they have suffered at the teeth of pike. Little perch will hang on to the tail treble with their usual gentle pluck, but pike *maul* this plug. Even so, the hooks and hook-mounts on our plugs are still good, but the dorsal ridge has little remaining of the original dark colour.

Floating Rapalas of the 160 mm length, in silver or gold, we found superbly efficient on the Sixteen Foot River in the Fens. They can be flicked easily under the far bank and on a rapid initial retrieve will dive not too deeply to catch on the marginal ledge, but sufficiently steeply to get well down by the time they are halfway across. Considerable lengths of the Sixteen Foot are over nine feet deep and the 160 mm Rapalas will reach at least six feet down even on the shortest traverse at right-angles to the bank. Unlike many other of our favourite lures, such as Snipers, Rapalas do not, on our waters, take many perch and they are more successful with pike than anything else. Although we have fished them in amongst some big brown and sea trout they have never succeeded, and yet on the big Irish loughs they have on occasions been deadly with big trout (not to us we hasten to add).

Returning to the use of Rapalas on the Sixteen Foot and other fenland drains, it is an excellent idea to flick them along the bank in front of you before moving on to the next swim. This not only produces plenty of small pike which dart out of the marginal soft weeds, but the activity of playing small pike commonly stirs the bigger ones into action.

Rapalas can also be worked slowly and shallowly; at least, the floating models can. The sinkers like the Countdown series are equally good as floaters, and it is simply necessary to get used to the sinking rate and diving rate for each one that you use. It is no good letting the plug sink right to the bottom before beginning a retrieve.

Normark produce one other Rapala range, the Rapala jigs, which is well worthy of mention. These have a similar shape to the rest of the range but are fitted with single hooks at the head and tail, and a treble hook on the belly. They can be worked off bridges as well as boats, though we hesitate to suggest that they be used in waters where there is no bank access to private fishing!

CREEK CHUB MOUSE

Several firms make floating and diving mice, in a variety of colours from grey to tiger-striped! The Creek Chub floater which dives to about two feet on retrieve is a superb lure. In all probability those made by other firms are just as good, but it happens that we latched on to Creek Chub's version in the tiger-stripes and have never looked back. Our first version had a 70 mm body plus a further 50 mm of stiff yellow tail, a black and yellow-striped body and a red throat. It casts extremely well, since although rather light it has a compact aerodynamic shape: casts of forty yards plus are easy with a back-wind.

This plug is extremely buoyant and it needs a fairly quick retrieve to get it down to two feet or so. The slow wobble is superbly effective. We first used it on a relatively deep featureless drain in Lincolnshire and found several small pike with it, and have subsequently used it extensively in the Fens both on the drains and gravel pits. It seems to come into its own in the same type of water as the Gudebrod Sniper, namely, shallow with a fair bit of sunken weed across which to retrieve. For deeper water it is better to go for a deep-diving mouse such as Tiny Tim or Mitie Mouse. Of course, the great delight in using a mouse is in using it near or on the surface, where you can kid yourself that you have persuaded the pike to chase a mouse.

HEDDON'S CRAZY CRAWLER

When Barrie first used one of these, on a flat calm lake north of Cambridge, he was simply hoping for a few jack pike for reassurance really: it looks such an unlikely plug by British standards. Anyway, this Crazy Crawler was flip-flopping its way slowly across the top of the calm end of the pond, with him watching it in fascination, when there was a horrible sound like tearing cloth and the faintest of plucks at the rod end. It wasn't his trousers that had got caught up in the brambles (his first thought!) but a *perch* that had hooked itself on the back end of the Crazy Crawler. He reeled in this fish, about ½ lb it weighed, and marvelled as always at the way a little perch will attack a large plug. They do exactly the same with Gudebrod Snipers of 4-inch length.

He went on to take several perch that afternoon, all from the surface, all in the flat calm water, and all took with a sound like tearing cloth. The noise made him jump even though he was expecting it, and he decided it was caused by the perch opening their mouths very wide just before engulfing the lure. In all probability they ship a fair bit of water at that precise moment!

He subsequently found that, in the Cambridge area at least, Crazy Crawlers are good for perch; that they will regularly take lures off the surface, but that flat calm conditions are not necessary for success. With pike we had read that a flat calm was essential for this plug, but again we found it succeeded well even with a chop. The only trouble is that the action is slightly affected as the plug gets buffetted around. But the pike and perch still gulp it down.

It is an extremely good plug for fishing over the top of dense weed beds when these reach sufficiently close to the surface to interfere even with a shallow diver. Both pike and perch will chase considerable distances across the top of thick soft weed to take the plug. Of what might be called surface crawlers and poppers this is the plug we have found most effective.

NORMAN'S FLASHAD

A lot of Norman's lures are good but, whilst the top-water Chuggerflash is quite famous, the Flashads seem to have been overlooked by most plug fiends. This is another shallow running, wobbling plug, and it looks somewhat like a bream in profile and is fittingly flat like a bream. The diving vane is broad, and the plug has a very slow wobble. On one fenland drain Barrie has had fish after fish on it, and the only drawback seems to be that the position of the trebles relative to the stiff, flat body gives the pike a fair leverage for unhooking itself – and quite a few do manage this feat. In fact, of all the plugs we have used, we have had a bigger percentage of fish come off with this one than any others: it also gets more takes than most other plugs. Heddon's Punkin Seed is a similar plug, but a sinker, and with a faster wobble. The two make a good pair.

HEDDON'S RIVER RUNT SPOOK

As far as British anglers are concerned this plug, and the various copies of it made by other firms, has been around a long time. In fact we can remember Bernard Venables listing it and illustrating it in books such as *Fish and Fishing*, and they were for a long time one of the few North American plugs widely available to Britain's anglers.

It is a floater, and with a shallow, wobbling dive down to a couple of feet or so. Bearing in mind the general tendency that today's plug fishermen have to use plugs that are too big, a general reversion to the River Runt Spook would do no harm at all. They can be dropped in the water with a little plop and the angler can quietly search the near bank and around the edges of weed beds. The trouble with big plugs is that on many occasions the splash of them hitting the water frightens all the fish within a twenty-yard radius: since the cast tends to be much longer than twenty yards this probably explains why a big lure often travels at least this distance before anything shows an interest in it. The River Runt Spook is often snapped up within seconds of hitting the surface.

Heddon also produce slightly different versions such as the Midget and the Midget Digit. The former is a real beauty for close-range light-tackle work: it is a slow sinker, has a 2¼-inch body (60 mm), and the colour we prefer is black with a silver-striped body and yellow eyes. It is also one of the best *hooking* plugs that we have ever come across, probably because the body is not much larger than the hooks. On some waters it proved excellent with perch, and like all black lures seems particularly good at night. Both the Midget and the standard come in a deep diving version, that is, with a big, almost horizontally-set diving vane carrying the trace attachment link.

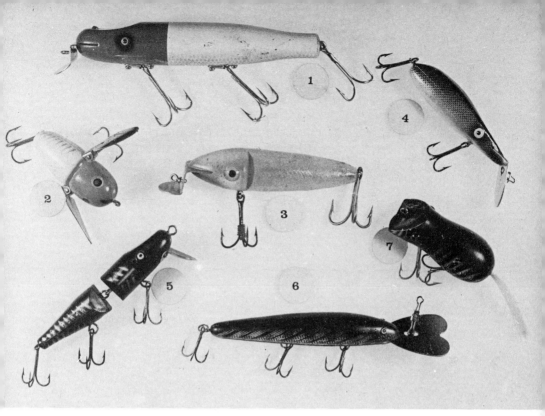

6 A SELECTION OF OUR FAVOURITE PIKE LURES. As you can see, they are well-worn. 1. Creek Chub Pikie 2. Crazy Crawler 3. Sniper 4. Cello-Dip 5. Jointed Creek Chub Pikie 6. Norman's Deep Runner 7. Creek Chub Mouse.

ABU'S HI-LO RANGE

We have, perhaps, always regarded Abu tackle with mixed feelings, based as it was originally on Scandinavian angling, but among the many superlative items they produce, and which we describe elsewhere in this book, is the Hi-Lo range of plastic plugs. No plug angler can afford to be without several of these. One of our favourites and one of the most successful of all plugs, particularly in the larger-size ranges, is the Hi-Lo M in the 40 g, 150 mm size. Four colours are available and a really successful one is that with a golden back and sides, with a greenish head and green outlines to the scales; the stripes and dorsal ridge are black and the belly silvery. The Hi-Lo range has an adjustable diving lip: set it at a low angle to the horizontal and the lure dives very steeply; set it slightly backwards from the vertical and the lure either dives very shallowly or pops on the surface depending upon the rate of retrieves.

When fishing the big Hi-Lo in rough conditions there is a tendency for the diving vane to alter its position, and this can be irritating at times. Of course, the older the plug the greater is this tendency. The treble hooks are attached each by a *pair* of screws into the plastic body, but the chances of one pulling out are about nil: it has *never* happened to the authors, although we have found an occasional screw that works loose.

Pike of all sizes take even the jumbo-sized 150 mm Hi-Lo and the terrific vibratory wobble can, on some days, be far more effective than any plug or lure in the box. We have taken as many as eighteen pike in one day, *in the depths of winter*, using either this plug or a home-made wooden version of the same thing. It is not our intention to detract from Abu's product in any way, but it *is* possible to make yourselves wooden copies of the big Hi-Lo but, of course, with a non-adjustable vane, and these work really well. By making a few yourself it is possible to extend the somewhat limited colour-range available.

SHAKESPEARE'S BIG 'S'

John Hennes, the Shakespeare rep., thrust a brand-new Big 'S' into Ken's hot hand when they met early in 1974. Ken closed his fingers over it, and refused to let go – it looked just about the 'fishiest' lure he had ever seen. Later that night he showed it to Alan Vare, who, after a close examination, vowed that if he hadn't just had tea, he could cheerfully eat it.

Not only has this plug some great sweeping lines, it has a tremendous finish, and is available in a wide variety of colours. The one Ken possessed was in a blue and silver bream-type colour, and in fact this plug looks like a very pregnant bream. There has been a great deal of thought throughout its construction. The trebles are fine wire, and not too heavy, a common fault with many plugs. Instead of the usual screw-fitting for the trebles the eye is an integral part of the casting, and would take one hell of a lot of twisting before they would give. Split-rings hold the hooks well clear of any levering hold against the body itself.

This is one of the plugs with an in-built sonic vibrator – a lump of lead that rattles inside the body for the benefit of the old-fashioned thinkers. We have mixed feelings on their ability to attract, though. The only way to really make them rattle and magnify the noise under water is by a very fast retrieve, and this is not that sort of lure. Occasional fast spurts, yes, but an erratic, swinging swoop with occasional stops can make this lure unbeatable.

Ken fished it first on the fickle North Met. Pit at Cheshunt, with success, and followed this with excellent chub from Penton Hook – the slack water, at the back of the island. Speaking to Peter Grundle (who is as great at freshwater fishing as he is at sea-fishing) we discovered another Big 'S' admirer; he (Peter) had taken six pike the day previous; nothing staggering, but good fish that moved on a day when nothing moved to other offerings.

At the moment we are planning a blitz on one of the big London reservoirs, and have marked this floating diver as a 'must' for the short list.

SINNER SPINNER

Whether the Sinner is a plug or spinner is hard to say. Probably it does fit into the plug category because the blades at nose and tail do not attract by vision, being fitted merely to create vibration and disturbance, or an alteration in water pressure that definitely attracts.

One of the small baits, we needed to put some work on ours before it was ready for service. The belly treble, mounted just behind the head on the cigar-shaped body could be turned via its screw-fitting, and we removed it, set it with Araldite, and replaced it. The screw-fitting at nose and tail had a very long shank and seemed secure enough – but we left it turned back half a turn so that the small metal propellers could revolve more easily. We also put more of a twist in the vanes of the blades themselves, and found that this made a world of difference in its action.

As a surface attracter this plug certainly sends out the message. The faster it is retrieved, the harder the vanes turn and the slight 'scream' caused by the water disturbance rises in pitch (see Photo 64 on page 157). As young Adrian Lawson remarked – the thing only had to dive to be a first-rate Stuka. But the steady retrieve is not its only capability. Cast and allowed to rest on the surface, then worked back in a series of jerks with a long pause between each move, and the rod tip swung back strike-wise, it produces an action that has scored for us with pike, perch and chub.

MR THIRTEEN

Ken fancied the large, wood edition of this plug for some time before he invested in one. Eventually he chose the Red Head with frog-scale finish in 3⅝-inch size. Everything about the plug looked fine; although the belly trebles were fastened in with a flange and small grub-screws they were tight, and the finish, as with all Shakespeare items, was first-rate.

Came the next day of piking and Jack Simpson, who was with Ken, decided to have a throw around the big private pit they were fishing. He dived into the plug box, selected the Thirteen, and started work. After two or three casts Jack let out a yell of laughter, and Ken looked up to see his plug floating away across the pit. Jack reeled in, and realised that the trace was complete and the snap on the clip-

7 Plugs from Woolco. Great value for money, and they offer an extension of some of our favourites in other colours.

ring still firmly closed. Watching Ken's mis-spent gelt floating away, Jack then proclaimed that if it wasn't so bloody cold he would have stripped and gone in after it. Considering that the plug had been purchased from his shop, Ken wasn't exactly thrilled.

Fortunately the wind took it across the pit and it was retrieved. The fault lay with the eye, which had not been closed tightly. Two seconds' work with the pliers cured the problem and Jack fished on. It was a day of high wind and biting cold, where nothing took either live, deadbait, or sinking plug. Jack had three good 'grabs' at the Thirteen though, but they were half-hearted, just short of a full-blooded clang that could set the hooks.

Some weeks later a Yellow Coach Dog finish was taken into service and this has proved a first-rate surface lure with both of us. The manufacturers describe this as a floater/shallow diver, but our success has been when fished as a 'popper' on the surface, especially over those large, flat and featureless areas that every pit possesses. By reeling slowly, then raising the rod tip *vertically* the plug will pop and skip across the surface like nothing else we've tried. The change to a yellow colour has, for us at least, been an improvement from the results position, and so ensured a place for this in the 'necessary' side of the box.

ABU'S SNOKY

Abu's Snoky looks like something out of 1984; the pointed beak, hump back and long, wedge-shaped nose caused us to rechristen this plug 'The Concord'. But it looks more like a fish in the water than many of the lures in our boxes, and that may be what really counts.

When first we saw it there were serious misgivings as to its strength. The two halves of the body casting are welded together around the whole of the outer edge, and at first sight the hook-mountings appear to be glued in with it. Closer inspection showed that they are fastened internally though, and a word with Tony Perrin confirmed that they won't pull out. Certainly the 11 lb pike that Ken has taken on his didn't leave any signs of strain.

This is another of the 'sonic' types with an in-built rattle. Earlier, we have commented that a hard retrieve is usually needed to make this type of attracter work – but this plug is an exception to the rule. Allowed to sink to its fishing depth, the gyrations this plug can produce must make the weight rattle, even on the slowest retrieve. Because the trace attachment is so far back towards the tail there is a very pronounced nose-down action that, when worked with a sink-and-draw motion raise mud clouds off the bottom, looking rather like a 'high' gudgeon freaking out. The gold finish we found especially attractive, and rather like an ornamental goldfish when the light hits the glitter scale effect.

MR MURDER

Mr Murder *sounds* the right name for a plug – and as every murderer is a one-off, so is this little widger. We say little, because that's the only size we've been able to obtain through our tackle sources – but Gudebrod plugs have always been difficult to get; probably because they *are* such good lures.

This deep sinker is a complete tail-over-head revolution. It looks like a very deep-set minnow, although ours has a perch-type finish on it. The trace-fastening eye is just above the nose itself, and the diving vane is fixed just under the tail.

With this rather natty arrangement you quickly discover that there is a tendency for the plug to 'lift' hard on the retrieve, and not sink as most plugs do. So again, this is a slow retrieve, sink-and-draw model that has, by virtue of its slim body, a fairly straight run that is killing for perch. We have had this lure so well taken that both sets of trebles, tail and belly, have been hooked well into the mouth.

A grand plug, one of our 'musts' in the perch and chub range, with only one possible doubt – the tail vane tends to provide a lever hold against the end treble, and could possibly cause a hook to free itself. But it hasn't happened to us yet.

PLUGS WE DREAM ABOUT

Among the many things, we hope, apparent in this book will be the two facts that anglers collect plugs in vast numbers, and that many

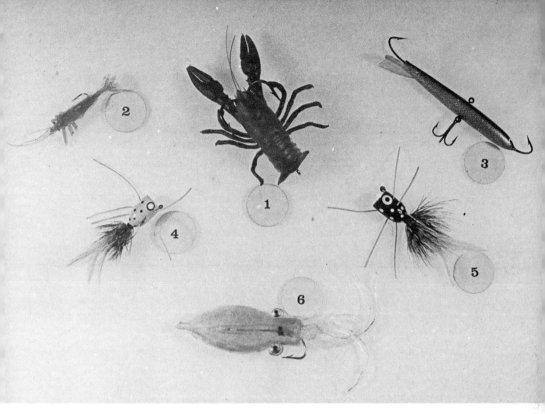

8 NEAR PLUGS. These we are still experimenting with.   1. Crayfish
2. Shrimp   3. Rapala Ice Jig   4 & 5. Bass poppers   6. Sea squid.

plugs are savagely adorned with treble hooks. If the hooks are to do
their job properly they will be sharp and oft-sharpened so that they
stick into almost anything with which they come into contact, including you and your clothes. If you carry many plugs to your fishing
you'll need a big box to carry them in, or else you might just as well
transport an armful of Prickly Pear cacti. You see the contradiction
we are working towards, namely, that one of the joys of plug fishing
is travelling light, and yet it seems necessary to carry a big box of
plugs if we are to get the best results in the way of fish. Add to this the
occasional encumbrance of a landing net, and you can forget 'travelling light'.

Or can you? Would it not be possible to get rid of the huge boxes
and yet avoid periodic acupuncture during the course of a day? We
have a dream which we hope will one day be taken up by the manufacturers. Something along the following lines is needed – assuming
acceptance of the basic principle that treble hooks and plug bodies

travel separately! This would mean that the bodies could be piled into a canvas bag, or into roomy pockets of the type in Barbour jackets, whilst the treble hooks, all mixed up, oiled, in quantity, and in a variety of sizes, could be held in a suitable box or tough bag.

Elsewhere in this book we have illustrated and described plug boxes and treble hook guards, but the advantage of this dream of ours is that the bulk and danger to the roving angler would be more or less removed. The disadvantage at present is that there are no suitable safety-pin type clips for rapidly adding and removing trebles to the plug body. What is needed is something like the illustration in Fig. F in which the clip is deeply set in the body of the plug, but until we obtain suitable clips in various sizes it remains a dream. However, we have already made some, using standard link swivels with safety-pin clips (Fig. G) as well as some using safety-pins in various sizes. The disadvantage of both is that the clips project too far below the plug body.

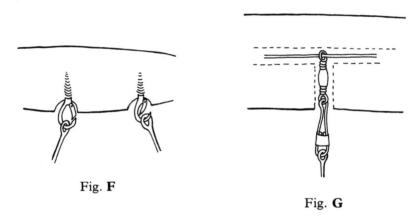

Fig. **F**

Fig. **G**

From the maker's viewpoint I should think it financially advantageous to dispense with treble hooks in the make-up of the plug, and just sell the body itself with simple clip inserts. Alternatively, the makers of plugs and hooks could get together and put very simple loops on the plugs and *clips* in place of the eyes on the treble hooks. In the meantime no doubt we'll go on buying expensive lure boxes, getting stuck on trebles, and extending our angling vocabulary with suitable expletives.

We should add, however, that Abu have made a considerable step in the right direction with their Kynoch plugs. These are about 4 inches long, one piece, and have an integrated link swivel, split-ring, and treble hook which goes diagonally through the head. The hook-cum-swivel is easily removed and the body can be carried loosely in the pocket. Another clear advantage is that when a fish is hooked it tends to 'blow' the body of the plug along the trace, thus giving itself no leverage at all: unhooking becomes easier for the same reason. On the models we have seen the link swivel is of the poor type, and what is really needed is a safety-pin swivel. If Abu can make a first-class plug of this type then they, or a competitor, could begin a range of dream plugs.

Perhaps this would be an appropriate place to append advice to those unfortunate enough to stick a treble hook in themselves. If the hooks are big, then go to a doctor with the lure attached (or unclip it if our dream comes true!). If the hook is small, rip it out with as little forethought as possible unless you think it is stuck in a particularly dangerous or unusually painful place. We've done this twice, on one occasion pushing back a little bit of flesh before washing and treating: it is far preferable to waiting for hours for the doctor to do the same thing.

4

Making and maintaining plugs

HOME-MADE PLUGS

The problem here is knowing where to start – not where to start when making a plug, but knowing where to start telling you! We could write a book on this subject alone, so great is the choice of materials and design and the chance for individual inventiveness. It is this last point, the scope for enterprise, that really makes plug-making a pleasure. And when your home-made lure succeeds, as it will, it is difficult to describe the excitement. The very first 4-inch, single piece floater that Barrie made caught a 4 lb 12 oz pike from the Glucose Factory lake at Rawcliffe in the West Riding: that was years ago, but you notice how the weight is remembered, and he can recall the swim quite clearly.

That plug was very similar to Abu's Hi-Lo Bo, but there is certainly no need to copy other designs. Think out your own theory, and then try to make a plug that works. Take, for instance, the Waddle-Arse (Photo 9). This is a big, two-jointed, wooden plug not unlike a Creek Chub jointed Pikie but with rear section completely

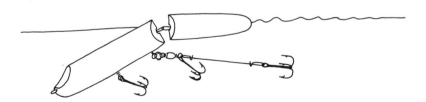

Fig. **H**

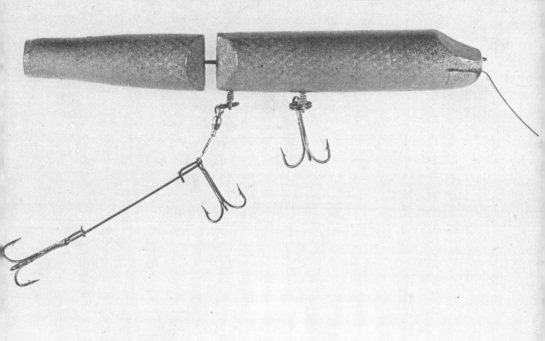

9 The Waddle-Arse plug.

free of attached hooks. The idea was that the tail section would waddle more freely without the weight of the hooks, and that the plug could be retrieved half-on and half-under the surface as shown in Fig. H. It works perfectly, and we are sure that when a big pike sees it (it hasn't so far, we hope), then it will not be able to resist it.

Had the rear hooks on this plug been attached to the rear section their extra weight would have slowed down the rather fantastic waddle. A further advantage, we hope, is that the trailing hooks will take a clean hook-hold and be difficult to lever out as the pike leaps and rolls.

Of course, one mistake was to make it so big. A good principle to get hold of when making plugs is to make them small rather than too large: it increases the chance of a small fish taking them thus giving you the confidence that they actually do work. But the Waddle-Arse is a winner, of that we are certain.

How was it constructed? Fig. I depicts the stage-by-stage building of the Waddle-Arse plug. Step one is to choose the wood, in this case a length of 1-inch diameter dowel rod or broom-handle in soft wood. Try to choose a piece with a fine and parallel grain, and then cut the two joints of the plug to about $\frac{1}{8}$-inch longer than you intend them to be. The next step is the only difficult one in the whole operation: drill a hole about $\frac{1}{8}$-inch diameter along the length of the head joint. We use a specially-made long bit and do the drilling on a lathe: this bit will drill a hole up to five inches long and if everything is centred correctly the bit comes out of the back of the joint in a dead central position. If using an ordinary hand drill or electric drill, the joint being held in a vice, it is better to drill in from both ends. The holes *usually* meet in the middle even if the junction is a little scruffy. It can always be cleaned out with a steel knitting needle.

The holes through the joint take the wire which will connect the joints and also hold the hooks. Having marked the positions of intended trebles on the belly of the head joint, drill short holes through to connect with the long central hole. When this has been accom-

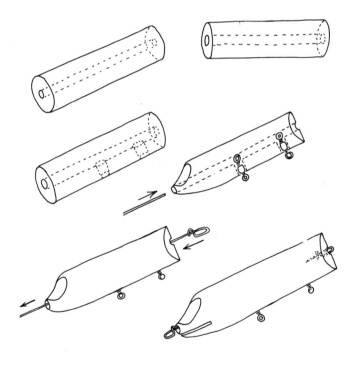

Fig. **I**

plished, treat the inside of all holes to a liberal soaking with a water-proofing agent such as sanding sealer, and allow it to soak in and dry.

Shaping the body is quite enjoyable. We use a coarse rasp and finish off with sand-paper of varying grades. It is possible to do some shaping with a knife or saw, in particular the chamfered edges where the two joints connect and which give the joints more freedom of movement. Make a saw cut at the head of the plug in the position you intend to place the diving vane.

The plug is now ready to take the wire and hook mounts. Push a large tightly-fitting swivel into the hole on the belly, so that a wire can pass along the central hole and through the eyes of the swivels. This *can* be tricky because the swivel eyes sometimes refuse to lie at right-angles to the length of the central hole! But it can be done.

The wire to use is stainless steel music-wire in the appropriate thickness. Ours is made by Ibbotson's of Sheffield and is available in 1 lb rolls from most large ironmongers or metal workers. Having threaded a piece of wire successfully through the front joint, cut it so that about two inches sticks out at either end. Using pliers, fold over 1-inch at one end and pull the narrow loop well into the joint. Then do a similar loop on the other end and, using pliers, slowly push the wire back again until a small loop shows at both ends. That at the head end is for attachment of the trace, whilst that at the rear end is for attachment of the second joint. When doing a normal double-jointed plug, as opposed to the Waddle-Arse, you then repeat this procedure for the second joint.

It is necessary to seal the holes around the wire loops to keep out water: plastic wood or Araldite can be used. The front of the rear section then has a ring-headed screw placed in the position shown in the figures, and a split-ring is used to connect the front and rear sections.

Attach the trebles by means of good split-rings. The advantage to attaching the trebles and diving vane before painting is that the balance of the plug can be tested in water and any corrections to the shape made with a rasp. The trebles can be left on during painting or not as required. Coloured hooks sometimes look rather nice.

On the subject of painting we intend offering no advice, save to say that scruffily-painted plugs often work as well as superbly finished jobs. Perhaps it *is* just worth adding that scale finishes can be achieved by spraying through a galvanised wire gauze screen. The whole can be finished off in a coat of polyurethane to give the skin some hardness, but with pike, for example, the paint doesn't last long anyway.

The diving vane is another tricky piece of work. We cut the slit in the head so that it will be a tight fit for the thickness of metal chosen for the vane. The vane will probably have to be cut to shape with tin-snips. It can be glued in position, or several vanes of different shape can be used with one plug, each having a different effect upon the action. In the latter case we rely on the tight fit to keep the vanes in place.

Choice of hook-size is as important as the diving vane to the action of the plug, and it is as well to try several before making a final choice. Our experience is that you always need larger hooks than you expected or hoped for!

Clearly, the above system of hook attachment is pretty robust: the weakest parts are probably the split-rings, seemingly a necessary evil. It *is* possible instead of the big swivels, to insert link swivels, but the hooks still tend to hang too far away from the body of the plug (see the section on dream plugs, p. 26).

10 Some of Barrie's home-made plugs.

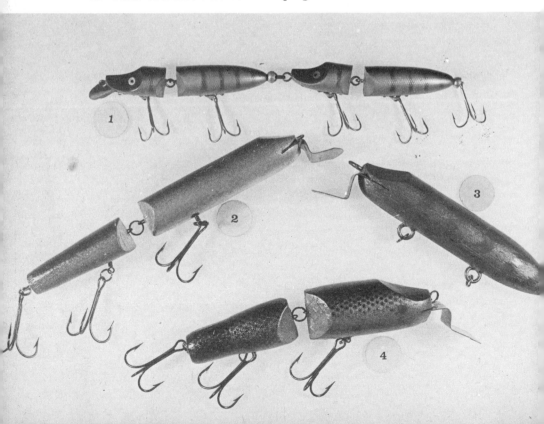

However, a much quicker if less safe way of hook attachment is possible. The body is shaped before any attempt is made to plan for hook positions. When the body is ready the hook positions are worked into the wood. All that is needed after this is a split-ring through the ring-head. Well, since it is so easy, what is wrong with the method? The main problem is that positioning the ring-headed screws tends to unbalance the plug and great care is needed, as well as occasional abandonment of a body with too many screw holes! Also, after a session or two in use there is an increasing risk of the screw pulling out as the wood rots along the length of the thread. However, if you are clever at positioning the screws then it is a quick method of finishing off plugs.

In the good(?) old days the Flap-jack type of plug was easy to make from the handle of a toothbrush. The bristle end was cut off, and the handle dipped into boiling water, which made it pliable and capable of bending into the banana or other shapes. Once shape was achieved, the plug was then cut to size, holes were drilled, split-rings and trebles fitted, and the job was complete.

Unfortunately, modern handles are made of brittle plastic and no matter how you heat them, they invariably snap when you try the bending exercise – or they catch fire. But it is still possible to find sheet perspex and other soft plastics that can be cut and moulded to produce some fascinating divers.

From the above it will be apparent that great variations of body-size and shape and colour are possible. But we have assumed that a diving floater is needed and that the body material is wood. In order to make a sinking plug you can insert lead into the belly of the plug, but this is certainly a tricky and skilful operation; it is easier to make floaters than sinkers. The great inventiveness of anglers really comes to the fore at this stage of thinking because it is possible to make plugs of plastic, rubber, fur and hair, latex-coated foam, as well as many different kinds of wood. The number of possible combinations is immense and it really would be silly of us to try to give account of numerous plugs made of differing materials. We feel we have outlined the fundamental points in the description of the Waddle-Arse construction, but the number of short cuts and alternative arrangements make the mind boggle. We shall mention specially constructed plugs at appropriate places elsewhere in the text.

PLUG MAINTENANCE

The best way of cutting down on maintenance is to spend a few extra minutes at the tackle shop. Every product has the odd dud that slips through, and although they are few and far between along the plug shelves, it does happen. Don't just accept the plug – examine it from head to tail, looking for tell-tale pin-holes that could be the fore-runner of leaks. Look at the diving vane if one is fitted, and make sure that it is fitted squarely to the body. Photo 11 shows two identical plugs with one incorrectly fitted vane that rendered the plug useless.

Hook attachments should be a tight fit and trebles should swing freely from them. Even a treble hook without a barb has been known to appear on a plug before now – and if the body mount is one of the moulded type, replacement could be impossible. Finally, check for cracks on a cellulose finish. Once this occurs it is a short time before water causes the cellulose to lift further, and flake off.

On the workshop side a pair of tin-snips, long-nosed pliers, split-rings, spare trebles and eye mounts, some Alasticum and Araldite glue will see you through most repairs. A little thin oil can ease a few tight situations and help to cut back on future work.

The pin-hole problem is one we have outlined elsewhere in the book, and it happens to the best of plugs at times. Before sealing the hole with glue, remember to shake out any water already in the body, and dry it. A touch of paint when the glue is dried off, and the job is complete.

11 Look before you buy. The left-hand plug has a diving vane that is out of centre, and is unusable.

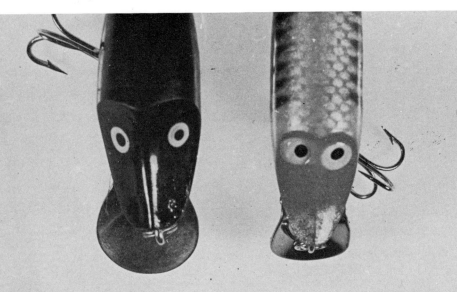

If, on test, the screws holding hooks to a plug appear loose – and this can be found on new or old models – they are best undone, smeared with a little Araldite, and then re-set. Of course, it may present problems if ever the hook has to be replaced, but at least it won't lose a fish whilst working.

Painting, or touching-up can be time-consuming unless you are an artist. One short cut is to use pressure-spray cans of cellulose that come in umpteen colours. Mask out with Sellotape that which you do not want covered, and remember to remove the hooks before starting, unless you want to colour them. With a little practice the colours can be 'blended' where they meet. Above all, do remember that because the plug may look a little secondhand and amateur in its finish, it doesn't mean that the fish won't accept it.

5

Plugs in history

Just how the plug as we know it originated is anyone's guess. Like Topsy, we consider that 'it grew', and was a growth between the natural fish and the artificial. When we look through some of our old angling books time and time again we notice the 'wobbled dead-bait' mentioned. At its simplest – and easiest – this was a fresh-killed bleak or roach, with one treble mounted on a wire trace that was threaded with the help of a baiting needle, from vent and via the centre of the body through to the mouth.

Cast and left to sink, a slow retrieve produced the deadly wobble of a sick fish, or if a little lead was introduced into the mouth, a sink-and-draw action that was fatal. Now all that description was to the make the point that the wobble was caused by the fish sliding down on to the treble as the water pressure mounted at its head during the retrieve. The bigger the curve in the body, the greater the wobble.

Let's leave those thoughts on the natural, and look now at pro-gress on the artificial scene. There is no doubt that man has spun – cast and retrieved a spinning object – for centuries. But, with ex-perience, it was gradually realised that an action other than the per-fectly straight spin could also be deadly. Perhaps a good example of this is the Jim Vincent pike spoon. Jim Vincent was one of the Norfolk giants who, in his lifetime, caught more pike than most of us have ever dreamed of. He used a spoon reported to have been made from a wooden original used by American Indians. It was heavy, long and with a distinct curve at either end that produced a peculiar wobble singularly appreciated by pike. For several years it was produced commercially – and in fact although not made now, the Creek Chub Cahokie spoon (Photo 12) minus all trebles other than at the tail, looks remarkably like it, but has a different action.

12 An in-between plug/spinner: the Cahokie spoon.

Now, somewhere and somehow, someone got fed up with not catching livebaits, or carrying deadbaits preserved in formalin that stunk to high heaven. At the same time either that same person – or his friend – got fed up with losing heavy metal wobblers on the river. So the wooden imitation fish that wobbled when it was pulled through the water and didn't get snagged quite so often was born. Or was it? Well, that's our guess, and anyone else's for that matter. The Ancient Egyptians used flies and it is not inconceivable that plugs developed at a very early stage simply by making bigger bodies for flies.

Early plugs to prove the point? The River Runt and some other American plugs have been going for some time, all originally made from wood, but generally it is considered that the Jock Scott plug (Photo 13) is the 'Daddy' of the English models. And odd though it be, it still takes some beating. Made from wood, with the trace attached to the lower lip of the diving vane, it is a natural shallow diver. With the trace clipped on to the upper part of the lip, and the addition of leads of various sizes it becomes a deep diver that can cope with a variety of waters. But its best asset is that the trace runs from head to tail fitting on to the outside of the body, and is secured to the tail by a turn or two of fine wire. When a big fish takes the thin wire parts, the plug immediately stands completely free and in this position it is impossible for a fish of any sort to lever itself free.

Naturally this innovation was copied, and 'improved' on by many people. Photo 13 also shows a 1940s wooden plug with fixed diving vane and straight screw eyes into the body. In the same photo is shown an original 'plastic' type plug that Barrie found in the collection of Don Carter of Cambridge. Compare these old-timers with today's products, and one can appreciate just how far we have come.

13 PLUGS FROM HISTORY.   1. The Jock Scott, with weight attachments 2. One of the first plastic plugs, rather tattered, but still usable 3. Wooden plug from the 1940s.

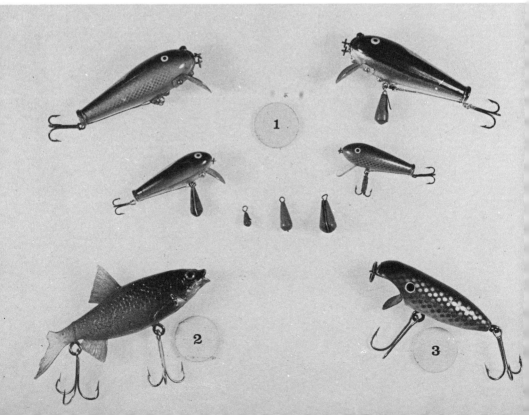

PART TWO

Tackle for plug fishermen, and general techniques

6

Rods

If you walk into a well-stocked fishing tackle shop and turn towards the rod racks, you can be sure of entering into the valley of indecision. There they stand; long rods, short rods, thick and thin rods, cork handles, plastic wrapped – each with a tag showing bare details of what the rod is, and how much it costs.

Naturally the salesman will take over, display his goods and try to suit you, but try as he may, and honest as he may be, he can only fit you with what he thinks is the best rod for the type of fishing you have described to him.

Now a fishing rod is a very personal 'thing'. If you go to a gun-maker and buy a good grade gun the stock and fittings of the weapon will be measured, tailored and designed to fit your body. This natu-rally makes for increased accuracy and comfort. Roughly the same thing should apply with a fishing rod. A rod which does not 'fit' the individual will not cast accurately – and can be guaranteed to be-come a ton-weight of discomfort by the end of the day.

Before you select a rod for plug fishing remember there are some basic principles which run something like this:

1. A rod is an extension of the angler's arm;
2. it assists in making a successful cast;
3. it assists in retrieving a bait to the angler's satisfaction;
4. it helps drive the hook home, and
5. it helps play a hooked fish.

With those thoughts in mind let's try to understand something of what goes to make a good rod.

One of the great games in a schoolboy's life is 'Whangee'. It in-volves a length of cane or stick, on to the end of which is impaled an

Fig. **J**

apple or ball of mud. A good heavy switch of the cane – and away goes the missile off the stick end at the required rate of knots. Wonderful for long-range window breaking, but of course it doesn't take long to realise that the furthermost windows can only be reached by using the longest practical piece of cane.

Look at Fig. J1. Here the cane is a few feet long, and because of this it will only throw a very limited distance; but short though the distance may be the missile will land accurately. Fig. J2 shows a cane considerably longer in action. This will throw a missile a long way indeed – but not with the degree of accuracy shown by the short cane.

Now substitute a rod for the cane, and a plug for the missile. The short rod will cover a short distance – with accuracy. This is the ideal rod for use in tight conditions such as casting on small rivers, streams, under trees or from a boat. Photo 14 shows a typical situation. The long rod will place a bait some considerable distance, but with less accuracy. Large lakes, big rivers, and gravel pits are ideal for this style of rod where systematic searching of the water will be undertaken. This situation is shown in Photo 15.

Now have a look at our schoolboy again. In Fig. J3 he is using a thick piece of cane, and the missile has not travelled very far, nor very accurately. This is because there has been little or no spring from the cane. Again, in Fig. J4 he is using a very thin, springy cane, and has not achieved distance or accuracy with it – the spring is just not strong enough.

Taking this one stage further Figs. J5 and J6 show the same effect achieved by either too large, or too small a missile on the cane. Photos 16 and 17 translate the diagrams into a fishing reality, and prove another principle – that weight of lure and strength of line must balance if a successful cast is to be made.

To help this 'balance' a fishing rod is tapered from butt to tip and the degree of taper and where it is placed can influence the punch that will go behind the cast. A long, slow, taper the length of the rod will 'spring' a plug over a considerable distance. A taper commencing near the rod tip will flick a plug over a short distance – with accuracy.

Now let's go back to the rod rack at the tackle shop and narrow the selection of a rod down to the type that will suit our fishing. For chub, perch and light pike work with short casting and small plugs we will need something in the $5\frac{1}{2}$- to $6\frac{1}{2}$-foot range. Such a rod will probably be described as 'single-handed'. You can be assured that the action,

14 A short rod for tight corners.
Barrie after zander.

15 Big rod: big bait: big water.

16 Out of balance. The plug is too big for the rod.

17 Still out of balance. A powerful rod and tiny plug.

or taper, will have been designed by the manufacturer to give excellent results – providing you don't try to overload it with a heavy lure or line.

For heavier lures and heavier lines a rod in the 6½- to 8½-foot class will be the type to look for, and for the real long distance, heavyweight work then 9- to 10½-feet will be nearer the length required. Most rods in the former category can be single- or double-handed, those beyond that length will be double-handed only.

The single- or double-handed tag refers of course to the length of handle. Largely it is a matter of personal choice, but there are some pros and cons that should be considered where the manufacturer offers a choice. Single-handed handles are usual on short rods and cast very accurately – because no co-ordination is needed between the two hands. They are lighter, leading to less fatigue at the end of the day, and by being lighter give a much better sensation of 'sport' during the playing of a fish.

Double-handed rods are usually long, and can, as we have seen from our diagrams, cast further and will guide a fish more easily than the single-handed effort during the actual playing. One final word on the double-handed rod. If this is your choice, Ken would advise you to make sure that there is a large rubber button fitted to the butt end. The natural tendency to tuck the rod into hip or groin during a day's work can have a painful effect without this protection.

There has been a slight tendency in recent years to move away from cork as a material for handles. Ribbed plastic seems the favourite alternative, but with what advantage it is hard to see. Cork is warm to the touch (desperately important on a cold day) and cleans in a few minutes. There is also less likelihood of the rod slipping through wet hands. But whatever material you decide on, do make sure that the handle is not too thick. Ken can recall one rod with this vice that left his hand looking like a carpenter's G-cramp for days after an outing. One-inch diameter is about right for most people.

Winch fittings to hold the reel in place deserve some thought. Most of the major proprietary rods designed for plug fishing have a locking device which ensures that the reel, once mounted, cannot work free. Usually the fitting is recessed into the handle so that there is a crank, or offset, which gives a straight run for the line between reel and first rod ring. Not all rods have this refinement, and where the winch fittings are mounted on the conventional straight handle, the locking type can often be fitted, but at extra charge.

Locking is usually achieved by a screw movement of one or both fittings locking down on to the flange of the reel, preventing movement through the constant vibration of casting and winding. Ken has a 'thing' about ordinary winch fittings that push together, and maintains that more bad language is used annually by anglers who have a reel fall from the rod at a crucial moment than bears thinking about.

The position of the reel fittings depends on the rod length. Usually it is well up the rod (towards the top of the handle) to help balance the reel. But that does not mean that the point of balance of a rod must be at the reel fitting. Usually it is slightly above the handle. Balance at the reel fitting tends to lose the 'feel' of a rod at the tip – an important item as we shall see later.

Ferrules deserve thought and attention. Split cane, solid fibreglass and some hollow fibre-glass rods have metal ferrules. Make sure that the female part is reinforced at the end, otherwise it will split. Also check that they are of the splint-end variety, whipped to the rod for extra security. Metal ferrules should be greased (candle or bees' wax are ideal) and not oiled, and a plug fitted into the female ferrule (when the rod is not in use) is provided to keep grit and dirt, which encourage wear, from collecting.

Hollow fibre-glass rods usually fit together with a spigot. This needs no attention, other than making sure that the small gap is maintained between the rod sections when both joints are mounted. It is left to allow for wear, and when it disappears it is time to cut back with a fine file the female section at the end of the spigot so that the joint will again become a tight fit. Spigot fittings benefit from a little candle grease – it cuts down wear and makes the joint less prone to slipping.

ROD RINGS

For plug fishing of all kinds you need rod rings that will not groove, wear or crack easily. Barrie has used a carp rod, made up by Davenport and Fordham's, for several years and the rings are quite ungrooved after thousands of hours of fishing, including a great deal of spinning and plugging. These rings are of seamless stainless steel, extremely hard, and are probably 'diamite', one of the hardest of all rod ring materials. It is certainly better to pay a high price for good rings than to buy the cheapest ones which are usually soft and will barely last half a season without wear. If in doubt, consult a good tackle dealer or one of the better tackle suppliers such as Tom Watson's of Nottingham or Oliver's of Knebworth.

Apart from stainless steel or chrome-hardened unlined rings, it is possible to buy lined rings either for the end ring only or throughout the length of the rod. The linings can be ceramic, such as Sintax or Regalox, or they can be Aqualite, a rather more glassy and more brittle material. We have rods fitted throughout with these rings and although wear and tear is minimal (Regalox does groove) the rods have a heavy feel and a softer action than they would have with lighter rings. For trolling they are probably excellent, but for casting continuously you really need lightweight rings except at the tip ring and butt ring, which can be lined.

To be quite fair to those advocating lined rings throughout it must be admitted that the range of ring sizes produced by the manufacturers is usually much greater than the range you see in the shops: it is nearly always possible to get smaller and lighter editions of those on display in many tackle shops. If the stainless steel rings are *really* good, it is possible to dispense even with lined butt and end rings.

For plug fishing other considerations than type of ring metal are necessary. For example, should the rings be High Bells Life (that is, well off the rod) or Full-open Bridge rings (that is, close to the rod)? Unless very fine line plugging for perch is being done, in which case high rings facilitate casting during wet weather, the low rings are better and lessen the chances of a loop of line taking round the ring supports during a full-blooded cast or a cast in confined circumstances.

It has been common for many years to have a large diameter butt ring, the idea being that it allowed the flapping early coils coming off a fixed spool to level out without friction. However, it has been shown in recent years, by Don Neish we believe, that a *small* diameter butt ring probably increases the length of the casts with *thin* lines. Apparently the slapping action from each coil of line unravelling off the reel and hitting the rod acts as a brake when large rings are used.

Spacing of the rings along the rod is not particularly difficult, and any tackle-making shopkeeper will give advice here. (In Cambridge, Barrie runs to Percy Anderson or Les Beacroft for help, whilst Ken has only to ring Jack Simpson). The only points to remember are to place the rings with Sellotape first before binding and to avoid an arrangement which, when the rod is bent, looks like the first example shown in Fig. K. Try to strike a medium between too few rings, or the too many which will soften the rod action.

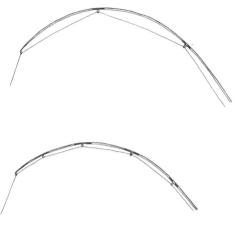

Fig. **K**

ROD MATERIALS

Something left until last has been the choice of rod materials. There are three choices – hollow fibre-glass, solid fibre-glass, and split cane; and each has its own devotees.

Solid fibre-glass is heavy, 'cold', and appears to lack sensitivity. It is the sort of stuff one associates with open boats and shark fishing. But this is not entirely the case, and provided one keeps to the small rod – six feet and under – it is only slightly different from its hollow counterpart.

Its main advantage lies in its enormous strength, and it really comes into its own when fishing tight, well-snagged areas where a tug-of-war to release tackle may ensue. The biggest disservice the tackle industry perpetrates with solid fibre-glass is fitting ferrules that would appear to have been cut from an oil pipeline. There are one or two makes with light but strong reinforced ferrules, and these are the ones to choose from.

Hollow fibre-glass and the word indestructible are synonymous in many anglers' minds. Fibre-glass blanks are only as tough as the manufacturers decide – and the best ever made will not stand slamming in car doors, stepping on, and other forms of maltreatment seen beside the water. Light, tough blanks are expensive and trouble-free, although repeated snatching at tackle to effect a retrieve from snags can, and does, produce a bend, or 'set' as it is called.

Fibre-glass may be rot-proof, but the silk whippings that hold rod rings etc. in place are not, and a thin coat of copal varnish every year goes a long way towards keeping a rod ready for instant use.

Split cane is making a massive come-back in the United States of America as a rod material – but tends to remain rather an 'out' in this country, mainly because of its expense. Rather a strange situation when you appreciate that Britain produces the best split cane rods in the world.

Make no mistake, a rod built from split cane is warm, light, responsive to the hand – but an absolute swine to keep if it is to last. Modern cassion glues have obviated the old habit of the sections that form the rod becoming unstuck, through either over/under heat or over/ under moisture conditions.

But the problem of 'set' can rear its ugly head in a split cane rod at an early stage, no matter how well you dry and handle it between outings. Basically this is a problem of strain, and a busy plug caster's rod is well and truly thrashed from this quarter throughout the season. If you are dead set (pardon the pun) on the stuff, then be prepared to strip and turn the rod rings every two or three years. This produces at least a temporary straightening.

Having said all that, Ken admits to owning a 7-foot split cane old faithful that has more years than he has sense, and looks like a dog's back leg. Every year it is put aside for the rubbish bin – and solemnly retrieved for yet another day. The excuse for its redemption? It may be useful on some small water or other.

By design, this chapter contains a large amount of very elementary knowledge. We have deliberately included it because the rod is a prime piece of equipment, around which all remaining tackle must fit and balance. It is generally the item of tackle most taken for granted by anglers, and the idea that any old rod will double-up for a bit of live- and deadbaiting, plus some spinning or plug work, still largely exists. Not always is this the fault of the fisherman – tackle dealers advertise 'Sea or Pike Rods', extolling the adaptability of a rod that will do everything beside a gravel pit, or from the pier!

Take it from us: plug fishing is a specialised form of fishing and it requires a specialised rod. Think carefully, and re-read this chapter before making your choice. And remember that in plug fishing you spend more time holding the rod, actually 'living' with it, than you do in almost all other forms of angling.

7

Reels

FIXED SPOOL AND CENTRE-PIN REELS

Very few anglers these days own centre-pin reels that are good enough to cast a plug directly from the reel, but probably there are still a few people around, ourselves included, who began fishing and particularly plug fishing, with a centre-pin. Barrie used, among others, a bakelite centre-pin called the Aerialite made by Allcock's. Now, you cannot cast plugs directly from the reel, but you can pull off loops of line from the rod rings and, if the artificial lure is a heavy wooden plug, cast quite a long way. So plug fishing and cheap centre-pin went together when Barrie was a boy.

Ken remembers the Adaptacast coming on to the market. This was a twin set of reel saddles, joined in the centre, that allowed the reel to be turned out of the parallel-to-handle position into the cross position, exactly like the fixed spool reel.

In fact the principles were the same. With the reel full to the brim with line, it was turned into the cross position, the cast made, and line pulled freely over the lip. After the cast it was turned back, and the angler could retrieve in the normal way. The disadvantage was line kink, which increased as each successive cast was made. Unfortunately, you couldn't reverse the drum to eradicate the kink action. Mind you, the Malloch reel made just after the First World War allowed . . . but that is history, and proves that there is nothing new under the sun in the world of angling.

A few people learned the Nottingham cast in which the reel was set spinning a split second before the plug was on its trajectory, but a better quality centre-pin is really needed for this cast, and the only reel Barrie achieved success with was a high quality wooden starback.

The centre-pin can, of course, be used in connection with plugs when trolling is the technique, and here one has the added pleasure of *playing* a fish on a centre-pin. It would be a good point here to mention some of the better centre-pins on the market: the Match Aerial, Rapidex, Trudex and Trentman are among the good ones, but it is possible that some of these have now been taken off the market because of the real competition from fixed spool reels. With each of these reels the angler *can*, with practice, learn the Nottingham cast. But Barrie's Rapidex, for example, is just that little bit sluggish to get much distance.

There is a tremendous, almost bewildering choice of fixed spool reels available. And unlike, say ten years ago, many of these are really good reels. Thanks to the efforts of some anglers, notably Richard Walker and Eric Hodgson, some firms include a roller in the pick-up which considerably alleviates the problems of resistance which we mentioned in the section on closed-faced reels. As far as we know, Intrepids were the first people to put in a roller pick-up: they had a cheap but good reel called the Elite. This has now been replaced by better reels from their stable, notably the Supertwin, and once again this has the merit, apart from its workmanship, of relative cheapness. The other make incorporating a roller pick-up is the Mitchell range. It is probably no accident that we tend to use only Intrepid Supertwins and Mitchell 300s: both have roller pick-ups, both have quick-release spools, and on both it is almost impossible for the line to get round the back of the spool.

This is not to say that there are not plenty of other reels on the market, and that they will not better those already mentioned in some respects: Daiwa and the Abu range of closed-face reels immediately come to mind.

A short while back we mentioned left-hand wind. What is the significance of this? Quite simply, if you are a right-handed person you need a left-handed reel. This is because the right hand is used for the most important jobs of the day – holding the rod, making the cast with a one-handed rod, or *guiding* the cast with a two-handed rod. The split second the plug hits the water the left hand can, whilst the right gets the rod in position, flick on the pick-up and begin turning the handle if necessary.

Consider the alternative for a right-handed angler: he makes the cast with his right hand; transfers the rod to his left hand after the cast; then with his right hand begins the retrieve. The *important* hand is involved with the easy task of turning the handle whilst the weak hand is guiding the plug and playing the fish! Quite crazy. Of course, most multiplying reels are for left-handed anglers: Abu, for example, until quite recently made all their fixed spool reels with the handles on the left, and all their multipliers with the handles on the right! Now they make a left-handed multiplier for right-handed anglers as they should have done years ago (see Photo 18).

Intrepids, in contrast, make *their* fixed spool reels so that they have the handle mounted on either left or right, whilst Garcia-Mitchell reels come in either left- or right-hand wind. In other words, they put just that little extra thought into design, and have actually listened to what experienced anglers have said over the years.

It is not our intention to describe in great detail all facets of casting plugs with a fixed spool reel but there are certain points worth making. For example it is *most* important not to underfill or overfill the reel spool (see Photos 19 and 20). If the angler has access to bulk spools of reel line then the job of filling the spool is easy: simply reel on the line until it is level with the lip of the spool, neither under-

18 The left-hand wind ABU Multiplier, which prevents 'cross hands boogie'.

19 An under-filled spool.

20 A correctly filled spool.

filling nor overfilling. If, when practising a cast or two on the lawn, you find the line jumps off at the slightest provocation, then snip off about 20 feet of line and you should then have it about right.

Incidentally, Intrepids hope to bring in bulk spools in 1975, whilst their associated company, Gladding International, already do them. Bulk spools have the further advantage of being cheaper. If you have no access to a bulk spool then the procedure for loading a spool is as follows:

1. Reel on 100 m of line directly on the spool.
2. The line should fall somewhat short of the lip when it is all on.
3. Reel on some backing line, or wool, until the level of the spool lip is just reached.
4. Take it all off again and replace with the wool or backing underneath.
5. The reel line *should* now come just up to the lip of the spool.

Obviously bulk spools are better, as they are for all fishing. When casting, pick up the line on the index finger of the right hand (if you are right-handed) which should be holding the rod on the reel seating and be positioned, therefore, directly over the reel if the rod is held horizontally. Take off the pick-up. The next job is to throw the plug with the rod end, at which time the force of the throw will flick the line off the finger with no effort at all on the part of the angler. The other method of holding the line, by gripping it against the cork of the rod handle with the index finger, is a far less precise way of casting, and it is far easier to accidentally hang on to the line too long with the result that it whizzes round your head like an angry wasp. Barrie once did this whilst wearing a bobble hat and the lure whistled round and round the bobble almost severing it from the hat before whipping it off his head. The resultant language was as colourful as the hat and as spikey as the trebles on the plug in use at the time.

When the plug hits the water the pick-up is engaged, but the critical thing is to check with a quick glance that this action has not imparted a loop into the line. To reel the line on to a spool which has a loop sticking out not only causes slight kinks and bends in the monofilament but seriously impedes the next cast, both for length and accuracy.

If you *do* introduce a loop unknowingly, then try a long cast into open water to free it: *never* try a tricky cast under trees.

How do you set up the fixed spool reel for retrieve and playing? There are two ways: one is to set the slipping clutch at something less than the breaking strain of the line and then drop the index finger on the spool when a take occurs; the other is to have the clutch wound up tight, whack the fish *hard* on a take, and only give line by letting the reel handle turn backwards. Most people do the former, which is probably why we do the latter.

If you use the method by which the reel handles are allowed to turn backwards, always make sure the anti-reverse mechanism is off! This is no more laborious than checking the clutch-setting, and both can be altered accidentally anyway.

This basically is what you do when using a fixed spool reel for plug fishing, but the actual precision of casting, and the accuracy, only comes with practice. It is easier to practise with plugs than with any other tackle since their very weight takes the hard work out of long casts, and their size facilitates observation of the whole cast and retrieve.

There are other wrinkles; do's and dont's. For example, try to avoid the embarrassment of casting with the pick-up on. If you do this the plug hits the water in front of you with an almighty splash, and all the heads on the water look in your direction whilst you try to pretend that a fish has just risen, or chased a mallard etc. etc.

Don't reel the trace swivel up through the end ring of the rod! It makes the next cast rather lethal at times. If the weather is rough and windy it is quite possible to do this without hearing the click as the swivel goes through the end eye. Not only is the next cast dangerous, but the lining of the eye itself may be damaged. One way is to use a large swivel on the top of the trace, but in general we prefer small swivels for other reasons.

When spinning in the dark it may be necessary to put swan shot at the top of the trace so that this stops as it hits the end ring. The earlier mentioned problem of loops is all the more critical at night and it may be that here the fixed spool reel should be abandoned in favour of the closed-faced reel, even though the latter is not so good for playing heavy fish.

CLOSED FACE REELS

You either like or hate closed face reels – and there seems to be no middle course. At 'face' value they iron out all the loose line problems that plague plug fishing in windy days when every second or third cast is aborted by the line winding either round the reel back or handle.

Casting and line control certainly couldn't be simpler. One has only to press the button at the back of the reel, and the line hangs automatically held against thumb pressure, waiting for the cast to begin. Once the forward swing is at its peak one has only to release the thumb and out goes the line. Winding the handle immediately collects the line again, ready for the retrieve.

One further advantage of the closed face reel is that pushing the release button during the cast immediately stops the line. This is not only an immense advantage if you see that £2 of plug is heading for the reeds on the opposite bank – it assists also in preventing extra line pulled from the reel during the cast from lying on the surface, needing frantic handle-winding before the plug can be made to move.

In other words, once the plug is close to where it was intended to land, drop your thumb to the release button, and the plug, continuing in flight, will hit the water with no slack line behind it. Of

21 Closed face reel, the Heddon 150: grand for tight corners.

course, some practice is necessary, but Ken has found this immensely useful in using surface lures for chub, where 'plop' and immediate action in a tight corner would be the only way of beating a well-hidden fish.

So much for the good side of closed face reels. Now, on the debit side. The main problem is line going through a rapid succession of angles. Think about it. There you are, stuck into a good fish, with the rod well back – and the line at the rod tip already at an angle of nearly 90 degrees. Following the line down through the rings (more resistance) it disappears through the closed face line guard, and turns immediately sharp left, through another angle of nearly 90 degrees. It then loops over the pick-up (90 degrees) and then on to the spool itself, about another 90 degrees.

Now think of the other types of reel in turn. With the multiplier and centre-pin there is 90 degrees at the rod tip as the line comes through, then it more or less runs straight on to the drum. Result? Little or no friction. With fixed spool reels the line has the initial 90 degree angle at the tip, and another 90 degree over the pick-up. But friction here can be reduced by a roller type bush on the bail arm.

So bad does friction become with the closed face job, that an element of risk creeps in without notice. Barrie first discovered and discussed it with Ken, who then realised that it had become one of his many habits. Imagine that big fish again. You hold tight, pump up with the rod, and eventually are leaning back like a strap-hanger on the Underground. At that point you have to wind down to the fish in order to pump again, and because line friction is so great, you tend to drop the rod point a little in advance of the winding – giving just a little slack line to the fish. The rest is easy to imagine.

Another bad point with the closed face reel is that the spool itself has for some reason or other – probably weight ratio – to be very slim. This in turn leads to less line being carried, and shorter casting. We have already pointed out in the section on fixed spool reels the friction trap created by a spool insufficiently filled. Therefore, if the spool is narrow it empties quickly, and friction sets in almost immediately the cast commences.

There are several models on the market to choose from, but two merit comment. They are the Abu range, and those from the stable of Heddon. Both 'handle' well, but one gets the impression that perhaps the Heddon range is especially designed for plug casting alone, and not as a double-up for general coarse fishing (see Photo 21). Both models have a side-operating knob for applying drag, but Abu here have a more sophisticated setting that is very positive.

The main difference between the two lies in the pick-up mechanism itself. Abu favour the floating pin type, whilst the Heddon pick-up is a circular piece of metal with a succession of small shallow grooves cut around the face, over one of which line will catch. We don't think there is much to choose between either method – each involves a certain amount of 'snatch', but not enough to provoke breaks. Probably the biggest difference lies in the price.

For easy fishing and very accurate casting the closed face reel is hard to beat. There is a certain care-free style about it that certainly attracts many anglers. But neither of us feel that we would like to tackle a real record-breaking heavy fish behind one.

MULTIPLYING REELS

The first multiplying reel that Ken laid his hands on belonged to Alan Vare. He (Alan) had wandered along the bank leaving rod and reel with plug attached laid to one side. Ken promptly picked it up, looked at the magnificent array of knobs, levers and knick-knacks shiny bright in the sun, and had a bit of a twiddle. From there it was but a short step to a good hefty cast – and the resulting bird's nest was just about the best ever seen in rural Hertfordshire. The explanation to Alan that 'perhaps the sun caused the nylon to expand a bit' was not well received.

For all the dials and levers on the multiplying reel, it remains a basic centre-pin that is geared for a faster re-wind (the revolutions of the spool are 'multiplied' as the handle is turned) with an added advantage in its ability to be thrown out of gear, overcoming inertia on the spool when a cast is made. They are ideal reels for the angler using a medium- to heavy-weight plug over middle to long distances. For really bad weather conditions – pouring rain, and especially during high winds – they are superb, and for handling big fish they are theoretically and mechanically perfect.

Having written all those glossy words, it must be said that there is a large proportion of the angling community that dislike or are frightened of them, although anglers rarely admit to the latter reason.

Most of the dislike stems from the constant fear of over-running with an immediate bird's nest (see Photo 22); a condition brought about either by lack of mechanical knowledge and care, or misunderstanding of the manufacturer's instructions regarding balance of accompanying tackle.

On the mechanical side it must be said that one need not have a degree in engineering to cope with everyday running and use. The parts affecting a reel's efficiency centre round end bearings (ball-bearings in better class reels) set in both end plates. Leading directly from one spindle will be a form of governing mechanism, usually

22 That springtime wonder, a bird's nest caused by bad reel adjustment.

fibre blocks that are thrown out by centrifugal force to act as a brake
as the bait nears the water at the end of its trajectory. A manual brake
is also fitted in the form of a drag, which keeps the spool revolving in
sympathy with the weight of bait used during a cast. Finally, there
is a lever or push button that disengages the spool from the retrieving
gears, used before the cast is made.

Correct adjustment of those parts we have listed, plus attention
to the general instructions that accompany the reel, will guarantee
trouble-free casting. Perhaps the easiest way of explaining our
thoughts on this is to take an imaginary reel from its case, and go
through the pre-casting routine, starting with lubrication. Most
manufacturers recommend or sell an oil of the correct viscosity. Use
that, and that only, leaving the extra fine and super oils to the casting
experts who are looking for added distance at a competition. Don't
flood the reel; by doing so you will impair the efficiency of drag and
braking parts, besides splattering line on the spool with oil, which
won't improve it.

Make sure that the line itself is not below or above the breaking
strain recommended by the manufacturer. Light lines will not run
efficiently; heavy lines produce unwanted and damaging strain.
Whether you use monofilament or braided nylon is a matter of choice,
providing your selection is not a line that is prone to excessive stretch-
ing. Many anglers have trouble in matching the line on the spool
with the position of the line spreader (where one is fitted) on the front
of the reel. The answer is to tie a small swivel on to the end of the line
after each outing, and then wind this up to the prongs of the spreading mechanism itself. This stops the line from running right on to
the spool, and subsequent misalignment when it is re-threaded.

Correct filling of the spool is important. When underfilled there
is an inefficiency because the rate of retrieve is slowed down. When
overfilled the line binds against the insides of the end plates, and
causes unnecessary friction. Also, take care not to wind on too tightly;
coils of line will cling if you do, again causing drag.

Following that pre-casting attention, comes the cast itself. This
can be resolved into one simple drill that need be done at the commencement of fishing only; ever after this drill, the reel will be 'set',
and should need no further attention through the day.

First, adjust the spindle so that there is a minimum of end play.
There is natural tendency among anglers to think that if there is
plenty of play, there can be no friction and that the bait must travel

further; as also the anglers who use both spindle adjustments for a brake. The minimum of play is the setting to work for. Then set the drag to zero, and release the spool. Now the drag is adjusted so that the weight of the line runs slowly and just – but only just – stops.

Give a jerk with the rod tip, and the bait should drop about three feet before coming to a stop again. This is the governing mechanism taking over, bringing the spool to a natural halt. Wind back until the customary two feet or so of line hangs below the rod tip, release the spool, and you are ready to cast.

Knowing that the mechanism of the reel is properly adjusted, concentrate on the cast, and avoid releasing the drum too early during the swing. If you do this, the drum speed will build up to such an extent that an over-run is more than possible. Let the line follow through – and the reel should come to a halt as the bait hits the water.

For those that think this is a tall order, let me state that Ken has seen Johnnie Logan at the London School of Casting use this method and immediately after the cast, lean his rod against a seat. Without any braking from his thumb the spool stopped without overrun the moment the bait hit the water. With practice, of course, it is possible to avoid setting the drag entirely, and to control the spool solely by pressure from the thumb – but practice is the operative word.

Quite often abortive casting with the multiplier is the result of damage to the reel itself, caused by thoughtless brute force on the angler's part. Imagine a plug well and truly snagged, and the natural reaction by many anglers. They reel down tight on the line, screw the slipping clutch up hard – and lean back. Result? Well, strain on the spool is transferred to the fine spindle ends, and this causes distortion. Ever after that when a cast is made the drum will not run truly – and the angler's springtime wonder, a bird's nest, must result.

Even if the spindle ends are not damaged, tightly wound monofilament is capable of distortion and even the fracturing of a plastic drum. In fact some anglers wind a fair layer of braided line on to the spool first, so that it can act as a cushion against this strangling effect of monofilament.

So whenever you are snagged, remember the procedure shown in Photo 23. Wind up to the line, lay the rod down, and take two or three turns of line round your well-protected forearm. Now you can pull to your heart's content without straining the reel or, for that matter the rod, in any way.

Looking over the market in this country there is no doubt that it has a very strong bias towards Abu multipliers – and certainly they have a superb range of models to choose from. In particular we like the left-hand wind model – there seems little point, as already mentioned, in constantly changing hands whilst fishing. Also the high-speed model deserves mention; there are many occasions when a little burst of extra speed can produce some extra special action to a plug.

Heddon, Phluger and Penn freshwater multiplying reels are rarely seen, which is a great pity. They have some grand engineering, but perhaps lack the 'follow up' in servicing arrangements that could be necessary with such delicate mechanism. Certainly, second-hand models that come on to the market are snapped up in double quick time, and command a high price. If you're really on a budget, then have a look at the nearest Woolworth's stores. They have two models that are heavy in weight, but certainly light in price.

23 Pulling for a break. The line is wound several times round the fore-arm, and the line pulled without any strain to the reel or rod.

8

Lines

As in the other sections of this book we shall have to hinge our advice on personal preferences since no one can possibly cover all the lines available. Rest assured that the lines we shall recommend will do the job of plug fishing superbly, as do the reels and rods that we suggested in earlier chapters.

Several basic types of fishing line exist: nylon monofil; plaited nylon or Terylene; lead-cored lines; steel or wire lines. The last can be dismissed, for they are essentially sea-fishing lines that are not usually used with plugs. Lead-cored lines are expensive but excellent for certain kinds of trolling, in which plugs can be used as well as other lures. With the speed of the boat constant, and a certain length of the marked line out behind the boat, the depth at which the lure is working can be known exactly: in general, a lead-cored line gets the line to the right depth more easily than other lines, and without the addition of action-killing lead weights. Lead-cored lines are not readily available in this country.

Most of the plaited nylon lines are excellent. They are usually less stiff than nylon monofil, less prone to being severed by the teeth of pike, and have much less stretch than other lines. With the exception of the Hardy range they are not now readily available in breaking strains of less than 20 lb: the famous, and excellent, Black Spider went off the market about five years ago. We would use plaited nylon or Terylene lines for heavy trolling of plugs, but not for casting from an anchored position or for working plugs from the bank.

The great problems lie with the nylon monofil lines which most anglers use because of their cheapness and availability. Let's begin by examining a couple of first-class lines, Maxima and Intrepid

Superline and itemising their good points. Intrepid Superline is clear but white and rather shiny in bulk. In water, however, it does, as the makers claim, become most inconspicuous and after a few outings any shine is lost. The diameter of 10 lb b.s. is 0·30 mm.; it is consistently round in cross section with no 'flats' or bumps. For its breaking strain it is, therefore, quite a fine line, and after using it for thousands of hours we can dub it a really first-class product.

But no fine line made is invisible to fish, and the only improvement we can suggest for Superline is to produce it in a dull brown or sorrel colour with a dull or matt finish. Dull objects are less conspicuous to fish than transparent objects. However, it is fair to say that in our experience sudden loss of strength in lines occurs most commonly in lines which have been dyed, so that the improvement we suggest may have occasional detrimental side effects.

There are still anglers who say that nylon does not deteriorate *suddenly*, but most would agree to a gradual falling-off due to the effects of sunlight and ultraviolet light. Our experience is that if a line is put under unusual strain, as when you have to pull for a break from a solid snag such as a log or a rock, then rapid loss of strength *can* occur. It does not always happen but we know of four or five such cases in our own fishing during the last three years: one trip the line is perfectly fine, and the next trip you find a 14 lb line (nominal) breaking at 5–6 lb. This has *never* happened to our undyed Superline.

A dyed line which is unusually reliable even with respect to sudden strength loss is Maxima, marketed by Milbro. This line, not as widely available as it ought to be, is usually brownish or sorrel-coloured after a little use and it remains dull and holds its strength for several years. We are using some 12 lb b.s. line which is three years old, although in general we prefer to change our lines each year. Maxima is rather thinner than Superline at the same breaking strains and can be classed as one of the thinnest unstretched lines on the market.

Stretch is a debatable issue. Many anglers claim that stretch in monofil is an evil to be avoided and recommend use of plaited nylon or Terylene, which have little stretch, or some of the very thin, non-stretch nylon monofils. Some of these are excellent – Platil Strong, for example, but others are merely badly stretched versions of the ordinary monofil. They have been stretched to a degree where any elasticity is removed. We have found some of the makes highly unreliable, and in any case we feel that plenty of stretch in ordinary monofil is not necessarily a bad thing.

When you have got yourself really snagged up using 20 lb b.s. line the degree of stretch can be highly irritating: you begin to wonder if the phrase 'pulled for a break' isn't a bit of an overstatement. Stretch is far less annoying when the fish takes you by surprise and makes a last minute bolt for freedom just when your reel has jammed/ dropped off etc. Nor need stretch worry the angler when long-range striking is involved: the good plug angler has his rod in the correct retrieval position of almost pointing the fish, and the resultant sweeping strike ought to be enough to pick-up over a distance of 70 yards to take out the stretch, and still drive the hooks home.

From the above it will be clear that we favour a thin, not stretched, dark-coloured monofil line. It should not be supposed that only Intrepid and Milbro make good lines, and another first-class product is Platil ordinary which can be obtained in dark grey as well as the usual yellowish tinge. There are, of course, plenty of others as well and in making your choice forget those lines which are stiff, bright and shiny; and at the other extreme those which are thick and which the makers claim are unusually soft and supple: they are, but you detect the softness best when tying knots for the *diameter is reduced* in the compressive points in the knots. Most quality lines are slightly hard and become more supple with use.

It is obvious from the foregoing that nylon monofil lines, unlike plaited nylon and Terylene lines, are more variable in quality. Much more care is needed in choosing from the vast number of types available: price is no guide whatsoever. Having got a good one, stick to it, write to makers to encourage them to keep it on the market (for several good brands have been removed); and talk to experienced anglers that you meet, since it is amazing what a concensus of opinion there is on what brands are good and what are poor.

9

Terminal Tackle

One of the great pleasures of lure fishing in general, and of plug fishing in our case, is that the terminal tackle is relatively simple. When working a plug for perch or chub, or even trout, it is only necessary to have a link swivel on the end of the reel line, and an anti-kink vane some distance up the line from the link swivel. The link swivel is simply for rapid attachment of plugs.

The only change in this arrangement that is ever necessary is to add a wire trace, for example when pike are the quarry. In this case the tackle arrangement is as in Fig. L. Having said all that it must be pointed out that most plugs do not twist the line very much and we often dispense, therefore, with the anti-kink vane. Occasionally, when using very small plugs for perch, we also leave out the link swivel because it may look quite conspicuous sticking out of the front of the plug! In this case we merely use a half blood-knot on the reel line to attach it to the ring at the front of the plug. When making bits of terminal tackle, or when carrying out changes of bait, there is only one item to avoid if at all possible, namely, the split-ring: never tie a nylon monofil line direct to a split-ring because the line will find its way along the split in five minutes.

Great variation is possible in trace wires these days, so it would be best if we explained our preferences, whilst not intimating that other types are no good. Alasticum wire is a widely-used and quite cheap form of trace wire, coming in two types, single strand and cabled. The single strand is perfectly all right for plug fishing unless you are in the habit of making jerky casts which may, during the flight of one cast, introduce a kink and almost simultaneously snap the wire. We think single strand Alasticum is best avoided.

Cabled Alasticum was really excellent wire until about 1973, when for some reason it appeared in the shops in a more loosely cabled form. Not only was the wire slightly thicker for the same breaking strain, but it wasn't stained as well as previously and it tended to unravel rather easily. We still use it and keep a small supply, but it quite simply is not as good as it was.

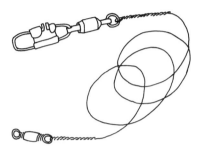

Fig. **L**

One of the good features of Alasticum was its dull colour. We now use Tidemaster made by Efgeeco, which in the 20 lb breaking strain category is actually thinner than 15 lb Alasticum. The colour is sorrel, and the wire stainless steel in seven fine strands. It has the slight disadvantage of being rather stiffer than Alasticum but that this is not really serious can be judged from the fact that one can still twist it with the fingers when attaching a link swivel.

It would be nice to see Tidemaster in 15 lb, 10 lb and 6 lb breaking strains for other uses than heavy pike fishing, but we fear this is not to be. Quite a few nylon-coated traces are made these days. They certainly look nice, are usually a little bit stiff, and the nylon coating doesn't seem to last very long: some are also rather shiny. But almost all modern wires for traces are so much better than the thick, black hawsers of a few years ago, that one can probably pay rather too much attention to the details of them. The aim should always be as fine a wire as possible, preferably dull in colour, and preferably soft and supple enough to make attachment of link swivels an easy matter.

Swivels in our experience are pretty reliable. All you need is a range of sizes from the smallest you can get, about size 10, up to about size 4. If you intended using plugs for shark at sea, as some anglers do, then you might go up to size 2/0 or one of the ball-bearing swivels.

Incidentally, Sharpe's ball-bearing swivel is of just the right size for use with 20 lb b.s. Tidemaster for pike traces.

Link swivels are more tricky. Avoid like the plague those which have a kind of elongated split-ring attached to one end: it is quite easy to attach your plug before casting, and almost as easy to un-attach it *during* casting. What you need is some form of safety-pin link swivel of which there are numerous forms in most tackle shops. In some the wire of the safety-pin part is rather soft, but since you can hardly go pulling them about in the tackle shop, only experience will tell you which makes are reliable.

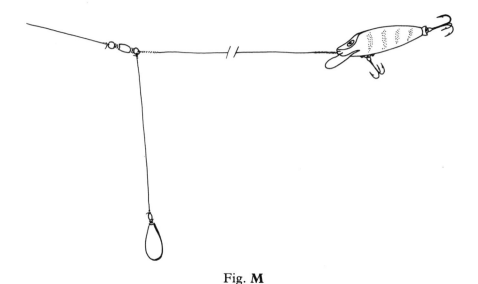

Fig. **M**

Anti-kink vanes are easy enough to obtain, perhaps the common-est variety being a simple semi-circle of clear plastic with swivel or swivels attached. These can be built into a wire trace arrangement. It may seem a rather silly point, but anti-kink vanes should not be simply threaded loosely on to the line or wire otherwise their pur-pose is lost. You do see anglers fishing like this sometimes, but such a sliding vane would only work at considerable depth where resist-ance through the holes might be enough to stop the nylon turning.

Other anti-kink devices take the form of half-moon shaped, fold-over leads. These last quite a long time before they crack along the fold, and are particularly useful where you want to add weight for casting or getting the plug down deep: two purposes can be achieved with *one* addition to the tackle.

It takes only a few minutes to make up a wire trace, that much must be obvious from the above. Quite simply, cut the length of wire you need, thread one end through the eye of the appropriate swivel or link swivel, bend back about one inch and lay it parallel and touching the trace wire just before the swivel. Then twist the two pieces firmly together so that you have at least half an inch of double thickness, twisted wire. If you are making up traces at home and have plenty of time, you can touch up the twisted portion with Araldite. This makes a rather posh finish to the job, but also has the added advantage of stopping the reel line getting caught up in the twisted wire.

That outlines the basic terminal tackle needed, but you will learn lots of tricks in addition. For example, our technique of fishing a buoyant plug *deep* in the Great Ouse is depicted in Fig. M. The line from swivel to lead is weaker than the trace or reel line so that if it gets snagged up all we lose is the lead. The plug, a floater by inclination, can be worked very slowly through deep water with a kind of sink-and-draw motion.

10

Miscellaneous tackle

The trouble with any branch of angling, or perhaps the joy of it, is that it needs a great deal of equipment which is largely peripheral to the main items such as rods and reels. Much of it is used only at infrequent intervals, but its use at those times can be quite critical in many respects. A good tip to remember, for close season blues, is to lay out *all* your tackle in the garage or on the floor of the lounge: not just main equipment but every small item. Then sit back, look at each item in turn and ask yourself a series of questions: 'Do I really need it?'; 'What is its use?'; 'Can I get or make a better one?'; 'Is there a better way of doing this job?'. Always remember that you have to *carry* these things. Usually you find several bits of gear that can be dispensed with, and always you find something that can be improved upon. In this account we want to give a personal view of the bits and pieces *we* carry and why: some will be carried in the vehicle, if not in the haversack or lure box.

SHARPENING STONE

What you need here is a small stone with a small grain size, say perhaps 4- to 5-inches long at the most, and not one of those huge, coarse carborundum stones that farmers use for sharpening scythes. Ours looks like an ancient slate (it probably is). The stone can be dropped in the pocket or left in the lure box, and it doesn't really matter much if it gets dirty: in use a little water will soon bring out the best in it. Others need oil, but most are reasonably effective when dry. After all, it is not really a precision engineering job that we are looking for, but simply a needle-like point on each and every hook.

The treble hooks on plugs get blunted remarkably quickly on snags as well as by knocking against the body of the plug, and since the trebles tend to be larger than those you would use on natural baits it is all the more difficult to keep a sharp point. But it is an extremely important matter. On several occasions we've seen anglers lose fish after fish simply because the hooks fell out during playing: and it never occurred to them to check the hook points. Other factors were involved, but as with motor-car mechanics, when you find one thing wrong there are usually other things as well! As with motor-cars, too, regular servicing minimises risks of failure.

THERMOMETERS

To put it bluntly, when the water temperature gets really low in winter plug fishing can be a waste of time. We know some waters that are exceptions to this rule, and if you prefer plug fishing, or indeed any artificial lure fishing, to other fishing, then you'd better find some winter plug waters in your own region. On one water near St. Ives we took, with some friends, more than fifty pike on plugs in three afternoon sessions. The water temperature was 38°F, but weather relatively mild for January.

As an absolute minimum therefore, a thermometer will tell the ardent autumn fisherman when things are going to get a little slow. Of course, taking the temperature is a little more important than that, since it can suggest for example when the prey might be on the shallows and hence well within the range of plugs: or the converse.

We use an Autotherm, a 4-inch remarkably cheap alcohol thermometer. Alcohol thermometers may not be as accurate as mercury thermometers at the extremes of temperature, but since we are fishing in water which is neither near boiling nor 30° below, this is not important – and you can *read* alcohol thermometers because the manufacturers colour it red or blue. Usually we tape ours to the plastic backing and then keep it in a foam-lined spectacle case. This type can be bought in large department stores, in tourist souvenir shops, and in chemists. There are many more sophisticated versions costing upwards of £1, but they are quite unnecessary.

BAROMETERS

If you don't believe in these, then here is one item that can be dispensed with. We do believe, and we use a small (4- to 5-inch diameter) aneroid barometer which is always kept in the glove compartment. We became convinced many years ago that in pike fishing, for example, a period of prolonged low pressure put the pike on the bottom, and scientific research on trout has tended to confirm this. For the plug angler, therefore, we need *high* pressure, or, better still, a rapidly rising barometer.

We are not suggesting that barometers and thermometers will tell you everything you need to know for a day's plug fishing, since there are the additional problems of wind and rain, sun and cloud, and water colour to think about, but they are useful in defining some of the basic facts of the environment, a combination of which determine whether the fish will move to food or not.

ARTERY FORCEPS

Most wandering anglers can be seen these days with a pair of artery forceps clipped to their lapels. Whether or not one likes this kind of exhibitionism is irrelevant to the fact that artery forceps are *indispensible* to the roving plug fisherman. They are better than long-nosed pliers simply because they have just as good a grip but are thinner, and hence are more manoeuvrable in the fish's jaws. Anyway, one cannot clip a pair of pliers to one's lapel! For us, personally, gags are not necessary and the only unhooking equipment required are forceps.

In bait fishing for pike our usual practice is to grip the pike's lower jaw in a gloved or cloth-covered hand in such a way that the thumb is *inside* the pike's mouth. The fish is then turned on its back and lower jaw pulled a little so that the mouth opens, and the forceps (in the right hand) are used to remove the hooks. When plug fishing a little more care is needed since the plug itself may be well inside the mouth, and when you stick your thumb inside it is as well to know just where all those treble hooks are situated. A pike's tooth will go into your fingers and then out again; a treble hook *stays* in because of the barb! People have been known to get themselves hooked up on a treble in this very way, and then have the pike start leaping about the bankside! They might just as well feed their fingers into the kitchen mincer.

Obviously, therefore, if you are at all nervous and if the fish will not open its mouth when gripped at the back of its head, then a gag could be used. In the case of trout and salmon, of course, the danger is much less, but since you intend killing it to eat anyway you might just as well kill it first and remove the hooks afterwards. Smaller species like perch, or toothless creatures like chub, can be gripped at the back of the head and pose no real problem to anyone. Again, artery forceps are the tools to use.

TRACE-MAKING ACCESSORIES

Pliers may not be all that useful for unhooking the catch, but they are useful occasionally when wire traces have to be assembled. Our system for wire traces is very simple. First, cut a length of wire and pass one end through the eye of a swivel, bend it back parallel to the rest of the wire for about one inch of length, then twist the two by hand, or with pliers. Then do the same at the other end with a link swivel for attachment of the plug.

You need *strong* scissors for cutting wire, so that this is one of the few items needed in the larger sizes: as a general rule most items of tackle can be bought in the sizes *smaller* than those recommended by most anglers or in the average tackle shop.

SILICA GEL

A small packet of silica gel in the plug box, hook box, rucksack etc. will help to stave off the angler's worst tackle enemy, namely, damp. One of the ugliest sights in angling is a boxful of lures opened after a season of inattention, and one of the biggest temptations in angling is to fish on with a rusty hook just because the point is sharp! The point usually *is* sharp, but the shank, or behind the barb, is very weak. As well as silica gel one can liberally sprinkle 3 in 1 oil on some items, but it is rather messy.

PRIESTS ETC.

We are convinced that trout and salmon anglers should have one of these, but elsewhere the occasional blow with a rod-rest is all that is needed. We only kill for the table the occasional pike, perch or zander in addition to game fish. We are not experts at killing things and perhaps the reader had better look elsewhere for advice on this subject. The only time Barrie tried to kill a pike with a knife he very nearly pinned himself to the ground as the knife slid off the pike's skull. Boy-scouts always carry knives it seems, and since many anglers are a little bit that way inclined, we suppose they do too, but it is one more item of dubious necessity. With reluctance we agree that knives do have their uses – in cooking, for example, carving rod-rests (not in plugging), carving emergency wooden gaffs etc. If you really *must* get one, then get a good one, like those Normark Vibro used to make called fillet knives, in a leather safety case.

BOXES

Some say you can tell a plug fisherman who is out on the banks by the rattle of the lures in his portmanteau. Others say you can tell a bad plug fisherman by the rattle – he is so unsure of himself that he takes everything. To which you can immediately counter that if you take everything you are sure. . . .

The point at issue of course is carrying plugs in the most convenient way without giving the impression of being a scrap-iron merchant on an annual outing. So perhaps it is best to start with the supreme optimist who takes three or four plugs only for the day.

Plastic boxes divided into partitions that can fit flat into large pockets take some beating, and the noise factor can be cut down if the bottom of each partition is lined with foam rubber, glued into position. A separate flat box into which traces, spare hooks and swivels, a sharpening stone etc. can be placed, and that is sufficient for the small-plug man. Small, because there is not a box on the market that can take three or four really big lures.

Big plugs can be rolled in a strip of canvas – in fact, Hardy's, in the dim and distant past, manufactured a canvas roll-pack complete with sections that was ideal for this sort of carrying. If you have a little flair with needle and thread it would be possible to make one at home. With a small pocket into which each plug can be placed, the roll can be tied off with tape and slipped into the jacket.

Other than that it usually means carting a big box. There are treble-protectors on the market, designed to fit over the points of a treble hook, and in theory this should mean that they can be carried loose in the pocket. They are a fiddle each time you are out, though – and things can go bent on you. Young Adrian Lawson, an angler who works, eats and sleeps fishing, thought this was the complete answer – until he lost a first-rate pike fishing on the North Met.

24 The perfect 'small' plug box. Note the Silica Gel and the sharpening stone.

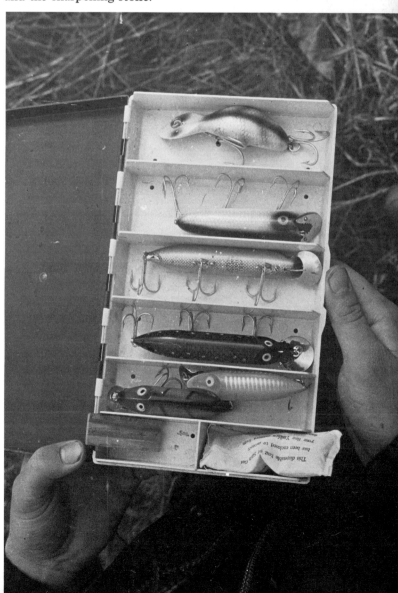

Pit at Cheshunt. When he reeled in he discovered that he had for-
gotten to remove one treble guard, hence the fish, not properly
hooked, escaped. We think that it was Richard Walker who once
referred to the buggeration factor!

So the only successful way to carry a small assortment of plugs is
to adapt your own boxes, and there are umpteen varieties of Tupper-
ware that can be divided up. Mind you, one feels a bit of a Charlie
going through a pile of boxes in your local store measuring each one
for size against your favourite plug – but shop assistants tend to
accept angling eccentrics. Talking of eccentrics, if you are one of the
types who permanently drops small boxes etc. into the water, plug
one or two of the partitions with plastic padding material. It works
– at the expense, admittedly, of a little plug space.

The final stage in plug-carrying is the full-blown tackle box, properly rigged with space in the base for reels, and expanding shelves
which are ready partitioned for the various plugs. There are many
varieties on the market, all of them made from plastic – which is a
pity, for this looks like becoming an expensive material, and today's
high prices are likely to become higher.

We have found that all of the models on the market are useful, but
that it certainly pays to have thoughts about the inside diameters
and one or two other points before making the final decision. Remember that because the outside measurement appear to be what
you are looking for, it doesn't follow that your plug collection will
fit the inside partitions. There is only one way of making sure – and
that is to try an assortment of plugs, plus a reel or two that you use,

25 Make sure that the shelves of a tackle box will accept a thick plug.

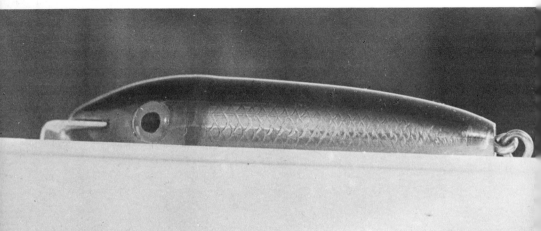

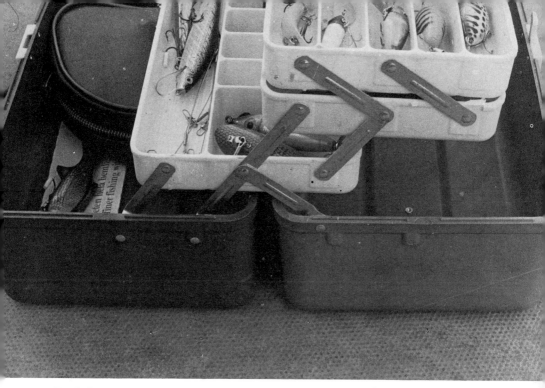

26 Both lid and base of this box fit firmly on the ground, and balance. But note also that the two top shelves are not closing because of a thick plug.

before parting with your hard-earned bawbies at the tackle shop.

Most partitions in the boxes will be found ideal from the point of size by length and width – but depth is another matter. For instance, try a Gudebrod Sniper and find how many shelves will fold flush over it. They are exceptionally thick across the shoulders, and with a treble mid-way along the body leave little space for manoeuvring into low fitting position.

Other small things can become very important; catches, for instance. Odds-on chances are that at some time or other you will over-fill the box, so that extra strain will be thrust on the lock mechanism, and also the hinges. Make sure that the welding of lock and hinge to the body is strong, or better still, that it is an integral part of the construction. The more expensive models, especially in the Abu range, have a safety catch, so that the lock cannot fly open at an inappropriate moment to spread the contents across the bank.

Another point well worth checking is that the lid, once opened, folds back completely and touches the ground. If it doesn't, the box will tip over once the upper shelves are concertinad backwards, with disastrous results. Photo 26 shows exactly what we mean, and it also shows an over-thick plug that will not fit flush into its partition.

There are some excellent substitutes for a big tackle box on the market, most made from plastic, but at a much cheaper price than the custom built article. At a car accessory shop Ken discovered one that was designed to hold small electrical tools and parts, and Barrie took to a toolbox from Woolworths that filled the bill pretty well. They need occasional adaptation in the form of extra partitions, but the handyman could certainly get by with one. The same advice is offered though; that you go to the shop armed with one or two 'awkward' plugs, and a reel, for a trial fitting before completing the purchase.

Neither of us have seen a box with a carrying strap and feel that there is a possibility here for the manufacturers to make a killing in the large-box range. Remembering how cold hands tend to get when walking on the banks, and how stiff fingers tend to become when cramped in one position round a small handle, a strap could be a boon. It would also tend to shift a large amount of weight from that small handle – a weak part of construction in all boxes we have seen.

27 A useful proprietary plug wallet. Note that there is still room for trebles to catch!

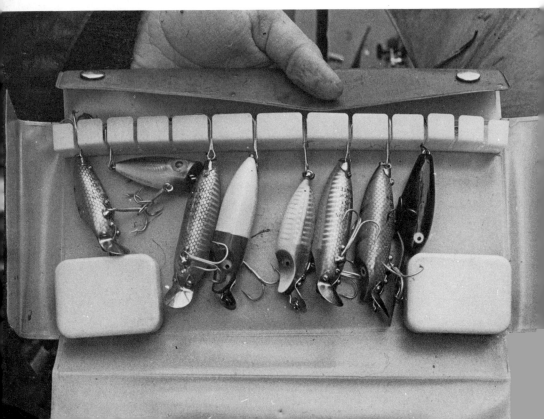

28 Vertical plug storage – the new box from ABU.

How and what you pack is a matter of personal choice. We both are united in carrying a couple of packs of silica gel to absorb excessive dampness and prevent rusting of hooks etc., but do remember that the gel-mix needs drying out itself on occasions.

The biggest break-through in tackle boxes that we have seen is the new one from the Abu stable. They realised that baits laid flat occupy two or three times the amount of space occupied by baits suspended vertically. A quick glance at Photo 28 shows what we mean – and just how neatly baits slot by their end trebles into the plastic frame that fits into the outer case.

The only box they have at the moment is designed for spinners, but Ken has used small plugs in it with success, and has twisted Tony Perrin's arm as hard as he can to produce a deeper edition that can cope with the biggest plugs. Despite its small size and large capacity, the designers have had enough thought to provide a body-moulded hasp, so that the case can be padlocked.

NETS

One day someone will perfect the ideal landing net. Of course, they will patent it and make a fortune – for nowhere in the field of angling is there more room for improvement than with this single, essential item.

Brief specifications of this wonder net are unknown as yet. But Ken would suggest that they could read as follows:

'Folding into a pocket-handkerchief size, and completely crushable. When needed this item opens on touch, and becomes immediately taut with a sinking net at least 3-feet deep. The sides are rigid, enabling a 30 lb pike to be safely lifted, and the handle is always long enough to cope with the steepest bank an angler is likely to encounter. The whole thing is immediately self-drying, smell- and rot-proof, and folds back to its original pocket-handkerchief size by perceptory powers at the will of the angler.'

All right, so that was supposed humour. But it highlights the problems of landing nets to perfection, starting with size. Size is weight, weight is loss of mobility, which in turn leads to fewer fish. It is possible to own an assortment of different sized nets – but of course the big pike always comes when you have anticipated small perch, and vice versa. So it is probably better to aim for the middle-of-the-road size, concentrating on construction and medium weight.

First, shape. A large round frame is ideal, but cumbersome. It can be purchased with four hinges, or made with three, so that it may be folded after use – but there is a tendency for the hinges to pinch the netting material, cutting and opening the top row of meshes so that the net itself will not hang fully from the frame.

One way round that problem is to fasten the top meshes by half-hitches to brass or plastic rings, which in turn fit on to the rim. But they will rattle at every step, and this can be a confounded nuisance.

Triangular frames are easier to fold, but the base of the triangle can present problems. If this is solid metal, there will still be two joints that can pinch the net material. Also, the netting tends to fall from the frame when it is collapsed, and in doing it will prevent the arms from opening properly.

The base section formed from leather thonging of cord is one answer, but it also has a disadvantage in that if you are trying to 'scoop' a big fish into the net (especially if the net is small) or land a fish from a strong weedbed, the soft base will collapse and the fish stands an excellent chance of escaping.

Weigh up the pro's and con's for yourself. We favour one of the triangular non-collapsing frames when wading for chub etc. or a collapsible net with a plastic-coated steel wire base that is held exceptionally rigid by tensioning on both arms for pike. Barrie has a very large round frame at all times – and the reference is to his net!

Solid metal, light alloy or fibre-glass are the materials used for frames, and each has some advantage. From a boat, where record-breakers can be expected and weight is of no real consequence, then solid metal is ideal. But for the chap who is walking the banks it is definitely 'out', and alloy has an edge in these circumstances. Remember, too, that there is alloy and alloy; some frames on sale at the moment are rubbish. One decent lift for a good fish and they are buckled. Solid alloy is the answer, and square or oblong in section rather than round.

Specimen-hunting groups have come up with a superb frame over the last few years (see Photo 29). The idea is that hollow fibre-glass tubing is used as side-arms, and these are wedged under pressure into the handle of the net. By bending along the sides they tension a protected steel wire across the base, producing a 'bowed' shape which is a cross between round and actual triangle, very large, and with great strength. Unfortunately, the design does not appear suitable for adaption as a collapsible model, but there could be a fortune awaiting the person who perfects it.

For wading or walking a collapsible net is a boon. Providing that the knuckle and locking mechanism where the frame hinges at the joint with the handle is completely fool-proof, all will be well. But there are some weird and wonderful creations on the market, not all of which are trouble-free. There is a lot to be said for a plain flip-over joint that is made from good gauge brass. Beware the push-button, spring-operated wonder gadget. The more mechanism there is, the more there is to jam, buckle and generally frustrate the angler. The means of attaching a net to the angler is also important. Look for the compromise between a hook or clip so strong that it breaks the finger-nails each time it is replaced on the belt or bag, and one that is so loose that the net falls off while walking along the bank. When this happens the angler will be unaware of the calamity – until crisis hour, and a fish has to be netted.

Often the hook or attachment on the net is suitable but the ring fastening on belt or bag is at fault. Trial and error are the only thing, and a little ingenuity with a pair of pliers can work wonders. From personal experience – beware elastic as a means of attachment. Usually the net gets caught on shrubbery at the waterside, and when the angler turns to find out why his progress is being impeded, the net releases itself and travels at a rate of knots towards his body. Nasty, dangerous, and painful.

Finally, there is the handle. For a wading net there is no great problem, except to say that we prefer something thick that we can get a good grip on, and that if possible it should have a hollow, or wooden piece, so that something will float if it drops into the water.

A present-day gimmick seems to be the telescopic handle on a wading net, propelled forward by spring action when a button is pushed, or opened by the angler extending the handle manually. It is difficult to see what is behind the idea – after all, when you are wading you should be close enough to manage a fish without requir-ing an extension.

Even more important is the fact that a telescopic handle is suscep-tible to strain so a heavy fish lifted with the net extended can damage the sliding parts to the point that they will no longer move. We are for the simple life, and happy with a medium-length strong, float-ing handle when wading.

For those who really need a long handle – which includes the bank angler not wading, or the chap who likes to combine both wading staff and landing net, a length of fibre-glass tubing is probably ideal. It is light, will float, and is strong enough to probe a pool you might want to wade. If you are an angling heavyweight who needs have something to push and lever with – then we suggest the proper im-plement for the job; a good wading staff.

29 Springbow net from Don's of Edmonton. Ideal in every way for that big fish.

There is a compromise for the angler who wants both hands free with a long-handled landing net. Here, by a leather thong and dog clip, the net is hung across the back and carried without interference to angling activities. When a fish has to be netted, the hand drops down to the side where the net is, slips the release spring, and the net drops down practically into the hand.

Our personal opinion is that this system is not only safer than relying on a collapsing net, but also allows a fair-sized rigid rim to be used. Beware the handle that is too long though, for it will interfere with an overhead cast – with painful results to the angler's head.

As to net material, well, present-day material trends are towards the micromesh. No doubt about it, wear and tear on fish scales are saved by this soft material, and every angler seeking fish he knows will have to be returned should use one. But micromesh removes more slime than does the older material.

Fishing for the pot is different, and it doesn't matter whether the net is cord, stranded nylon, or micromesh under these circumstances. What is vitally important is that the net should sink, and a small-bore lead bullet stitched into the base of a landing net will make sure this does happen.

Two final thoughts before leaving the subject of netting. Remember that the net itself is replaceable. Some of the slime-stiffened, mesh-broken smelly objects that one sees are neither practical nor necessary. Ken recently spoke to someone in a fishing pub about the smell from his net. The immediate reply was that it gave 'character'. Ken's suggestion that perhaps he should wear a Davy Crockett hat was not well received. Last, but by no means least: when the chips are down, the fish is beaten and being pulled towards the angler ready for landing – then, at that moment, the best thing in the world is a really deep net – at least 3-feet from rim to base.

How to use the net? Well, everyone knows that. Haven't angling books for years been churning out the 'sink the net and draw the fish over it' doctrine? There is no doubt that is the correct way, but only if the fish will fit into the net itself, and the water is absolutely still.

30 One of our favourite net shapes. Simple, but a little on the light side.

Running water requires some thought. That lead bullet stitched into the bottom of the net will be great for holding the bag down where there is only a moderate current. But as the force of water increases, so the tendency arises for the net to be washed back out through the rim. From here disaster is inevitable, and there is only one way to prevent it happening. First, play your fish to an absolute standstill, then face upstream, and enter the net at an angle of 45 degrees into the water, so that the current drives the netting straight out behind the rim. Then draw the fish upstream to the limit of the rod-length, and allow him to drift down into the net itself.

It all sounds rather complicated, but keep in mind the fact that the net must be streamed out behind the frame and that, gently handled, a completely beaten fish is a very viable proposition, and you won't go far wrong. It would be no exaggeration to state that three-quarters of all fish netted are not played out, and therein lies the cause of the failure rate at the netting stage of all, not just small, fish.

Ken has a colleague who has a different approach. Whenever he stops to use his rod he drops the net pointing out from the bank into the water at his feet. Then, when it is settled on the bottom, he fishes. Once a fish requires landing he has only to pick up the net as the fish is brought over it, and providing he moves quickly enough, the net will remain behind the frame during the netting. Disadvantages? Yes, of course, if the bank shelves steeply then the net slips off into deep water. Also, we don't much like stooping very low with a fish on a short line; this is how breaks are made. Finally, consider the wearisome return journey to collect the net you forgot. But for what it is worth, there is one idea.

So much for the still and running water approach. Now, what about the fish that is too large (D.V.) for the net? Well, it's either heads or tails. Once one end or the other is into the frame you can only hope that the bag of the net will be enough to contain at least the bigger portion of weight so that the whole thing can be safely lifted.

Which end? Well, for us it is the tail end into the net every time. Yes, we can hear the howls of the experts enlarging on the theme that with the tail a fish can expend leverage, and possibly jump free. But let Ken tell you this story.

A young angler was salmon fishing on the Towy in Wales. The lure – a River Runt with trebles at belly and tail. It had rained, and on the fifth cast the angler ever made in salmon fishing he was into a real old–fashioned rod–bender that jumped – but you have read all that sort of stuff before.

Finally the angler (perhaps we would be nearer the truth to have said 'young impecunious angler') went for the net. It was woefully inadequate and even allowing for the exaggeration of a first fish, there was a good half of the body that would never fit. So accordingly, and in deference to the good books and pundits, the angler sank the net, and drew the fish head first over the rim.

But even as it slid halfway the treble at the plug's belly caught in the netting and as if by telepathy the fish lunged. Yes, you can guess the rest. That caught treble was the lever needed and away went Ken's first salmon. He is not ashamed to say that he sat down on the ground and cried!

So for us it is tail first every time in plug fishing – but would repeat the early proviso that a fish must be played right out before any thoughts of netting with a small net are entertained.

In the net is half the battle, out on to the bank is the other. Let's face it, no landing net is designed to withstand a dead weight lift of 20 lb or so. Or if it is, there will be two men and a boy walking after the angler carrying it. Which reminds us of the incident witnessed on the Royalty, where two anglers were seen driving the end of an eight-foot collapsible landing net handle against the road bridge. One of the two had landed an 8 lb barbel with the handle fully extended, by lifting the shaft at its extreme end. The result was obvious; there was such a bow in the shaft that eventually, despite hammering, the two lads were obliged to drive back to London with the thing sticking out of the window.

Once that big 'un is in the net, lay the rod down on the bank, in the water, or tuck the butt into the top of your wader. Then go hand over hand down the shaft, and grip both sides of the rim or net with each hand. Then lift, and walk well back before you put the weight down – it's amazing how far a fish can 'bounce'.

GAFFS

If we had a large salmon played out, or the new British record pike under our rod tip, and considering the subsequent rage and exasperation if either were lost then – and under those circumstances only – would we reach for a gaff. In other words, we don't like them, and at best consider their use a necessary evil.

This, of course, may be taken by many as a sign of either sensitivity or senility; but it's not just the dislike of drawing cold steel into a fish – it is the fact that so many fish are gaffed where there is no need whatsoever. In fact the gaff, to many anglers, is a status symbol. Large gaffs sometimes hang from very small bodies, and at the slightest sign of a fish, irrespective of size, out it comes and in it goes. Fair enough – the fish is often returned, but with what unnecessary damage!

What are the essentials of a good gaff? Strength first and foremost. Those that are cheap, finish up being repaired first. Think of the strain on a gaff used to lift a 25 lb lead weight with a 'straight' lift, and you will understand a little of the wear put on to its various parts. Now bear in mind that in the excitement of the moment few people really give a straight lift – and you can really appreciate the strain put not only on the hook, but also the shaft of the instrument itself.

Steel and brass are the only materials that can take that sort of use, definitely not alloy. Weight and strength are synonymous in this

31 Hardy's telescopic gaff. Note the point protector attached to the shaft.

case. A good gaff extends to $3\frac{1}{2}$ feet, in two or three telescopic exten-
sions, the handle being of solid construction and the top solid steel
(see the example included in Photo 31). Pike gaffs should be as in Fig.
N since the intention is *not* to stab the fish but to lift it clear of the
water in good condition. The V-shape lessens the chances of the
pike levering itself off the bend. With salmon a V-shape would be
useless, since very little penetration of the flank would be made.

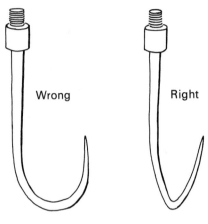

Wrong   Right

Fig. **N**

Looking at gaffs as a whole, our complaints lie in the protective
sheath that so often fails to cover the point when it is collapsed, and
with the hand grip, for we have yet to find a collapsible gaff that has
a leather loop for wrist security. We are aware that such a loop could
be added by the individual, but feel that it would be better incor-
porated in the construction stage.

The traditional gaff head whipped to a strong pole is fine for the
gillie, but cumbersome and a menace when carried by the roving
fisherman. No matter how one tries to retain it, by the end of the day
the cork protective covering on the point is missing, with painful
results.

Where to gaff (the fish, that is) leaves a choice of chin or mid-way
along the body. Most books refer to the 'point of balance' when
gaffing salmon – but in the general excitement of this final act, most
people badly misjudge. Ken has vivid recollections of poaching a
large salmon at night when the point of balance was misjudged, and

as the fish came out of the water it 'whipped', with the result that the poacher concerned took a full toss into the river.

A sharp point, the point of the chin, a straight lift – and the job is done – providing that the fish is properly played out.

TAILERS

Not often remembered, and usually associated with game fishing, the tailer is a sophisticated form of the rabbit snare on a pole used by keepers for ridding waters of pike. The principle is that the open wire loop is slid over the tail, and then the pole is jerked up and back towards the angler, so that the wire tightens around the wrist behind the tail, lifting the fish from the water.

They are fine for big salmon, and with sensible use do not inflict as much damage as a gaff. The main disadvantage is that the pole and loop are clumsy and heavy to carry around, and of course the pike has little or no wrist on which to get a grip. Weighing it up with the pros and cons we feel happier with the net or gaff.

BEACHING AND HANDING A FISH

If you are caught without the means of landing (and should it happen, it serves you right!) then your only resort will be to beach the fish if there is a convenient place, or to try and lift him out by hand.

To be successful, beaching requires the fish to be played until he is more tired than usual. When this point is reached, walk or climb round to the point where you intend to do the landing. Lift the fish so that his head is out of the water, and then, without giving line from the reel, walk backwards, drawing the fish firmly, quickly and very smoothly back with you, as shown in Photo 32.

As he hits the beach there will usually be a kick, and this helps to get the carcass just that little further up from the water's edge. Then it is a question of drop the rod, run forward and grab – and may the Lord have mercy on your fingers should it be a big pike: it's not the teeth you should worry about, but flying trebles.

Handing a fish – lifting it out of the water by the tail – is quite a

32 Beaching a well played-out pike.

practical proposition at any time. Barrie showed Ken how it should
be done with one of his (Ken's) best gloves some time ago. Unfortunately he left the glove under the dashboard of his van for a couple
of days, and when the door was opened the smell was a trifle over-
powering.

Use a woollen glove, play the fish to a standstill, grasp the tail at
the wrist (such as there is with a pike) and lift, or rather drag if there is
any size to the fish. Ken would, however, suggest a small plastic bag
if the glove is to be carried as a regular feature. Pike up to round about
double figures can be grasped at the back of the head with the left
hand, but when much heavier than this great strength is required
and it is far better to beach the fish if possible. When plug fishing
any handling technique must be done with great care, for a sudden
lunge on the part of a pike can drive a treble hook deep into the
angler's hand.

11

Casting

In casting, more can be learned by watching than by reading. This chapter is therefore devoted to illustrations, explanatory captions and minimal text. Barrie posed for the photographs very nicely.

> (Note from K.W.: The choice of model caused some bickering but it is clear to me, as his co-author, that Barrie wished to correct any misunderstanding arising out of the personal reference to him on page 85.)

33 CASTING WITH A TWO-HANDED ROD. The grip, arms spread shoulder width, middle finger of the right hand controlling the line from the reel.

34 Commencement of the two-handed cast. Feet comfortably spread, the angler facing the direction of the cast.

35 Power. Both left and right arm work in a sweep to bring the rod over the angler's shoulder. The line is released at the centre of the stroke.

Photos 33, 34, 35 and 36 illustrate the use of the heavier type of double-handed rod referred to on page 48. With practice, accurate casts can be made over considerable distances.

36 Follow-through. The rod is held in this position until the plug touches the water.

37 THE OVERHEAD CAST WITH A SINGLE-HANDED ROD. From a position of 1 o'clock the rod is brought vertically over the angler's shoulder, driving the plug out. The line is released at the 11 o'clock position.

38 Follow-through. With the rod held above the water-level, the angler can watch the reel and check the accuracy of the cast at the same time.

Photos 37 and 38, on the left, illustrate the overhead cast with a single-handed rod. The point of line release is very important.

Is there no limit to the man's versatility? In Photos 39, 40 and 41 our model demonstrates three stages of the left-hand swing.

Finally, in Photos 42 and 43, Barrie exhibits a more sophisticated use of a skill he acquired some years earlier.

39 CASTING FROM THE LEFT HAND-SIDE SWING. Useful for tight corners. The picture shows the commencement of the cast.

40 Swing-through and the line release.

41 Follow-through, watching both the reel and the plug.

42 CATAPULT CAST. Ideal for small holes in tree-lined banks etc. Maximum tension is followed by the release of plug and line.

43 The moment of release.

12

Boat fishing and echo-sounding

Wandering along the bankside casting a plug into likely holes between the weed beds, and carrying little but a net and pocketful of lures, is a delightful way of spending a morning, but boat fishing also has its charms. In terms of reaching swims not accessible from the bank it is often a highly practical way of fishing, even with a small boat on small waters.

It is not our intention to discuss the type of boat needed. The trouble is that most anglers have to make do with what is actually available, and in most instances these craft are not specifically designed for anglers, let alone the man carrying several rods and hundreds of lures. Generally speaking, large lochs need a clinker-built boat upwards of twelve feet in length. Some modern fibre-glass boats are also good, but whether wood or glass we are relatively unhappy on big waters if we do not have a good outboard motor, chosen for the size of the boat, and a sound pair of oars.

Certain other items make for more enjoyable fishing. For example two good, heavy anchors (one at the bows and one in the stern) attached to more rope than you are likely to need, mean that you can anchor in almost any position relative to the snags or ledges you intend working. The rope should be thick, not clothes-line thickness, for with the latter it may be difficult to pull a heavy weight out of the mud. Another bad feature of boats, from the angler's point of view, is the pair of rowlocks. Rowlocks are almost universal, and whilst suitable for the *rowing* enthusiast, enabling him to make quite intricate manoeuvres, all they do for the angler is increase the risk of the oars being lost. Now the Irish are not noted for their efficiency in most matters, but on this question of oar attachment they are 'spot on':

they have a block of wood on the side of each oar, and the block has a hole through it which fits over a pin sticking up on the gunwhale. Sophisticated versions have a locking nut which screws on to the top of the pin.

Using this system of oar attachment one can, in the event of a take whilst trolling, or in the event of spotting a big fish, drop the oars without a second thought and attend to the more important matter of fishing.

44 Plug fishing from a boat. Barrie, with boat set out, ready to go.

It might be a good idea to outline the kind of real situation that arises. Suppose the angler is rowing gently towards the sunken tree (Fig. O) around which he intends working his plugs, and having previously established the position of the tree, the suggested approach is as follows. First, approach downwind rowing gently and quietly, and if the wind is moderate cease rowing about ten to fifteen yards short of the distance from which you intend casting. Drop the oars and, without rocking the boat, move into the bows and drop the bow anchor gently overboard. Hold it on a tight line after it hits the bottom and allow the stern to swing round as shown in the drawing. Make the anchor rope fast, having judged the amount of line to let out in relation to the wind strength. Move gently to the stern, wait until the stern is pointing to the sunken tree, and then lower the second anchor. With the bows pointing into the wind in this way, and with two anchors firmly fixed, the angler can work the plugs past the snags in the knowledge that the boat is fairly static – or to put it another way, the sunken tree will not move between casts!

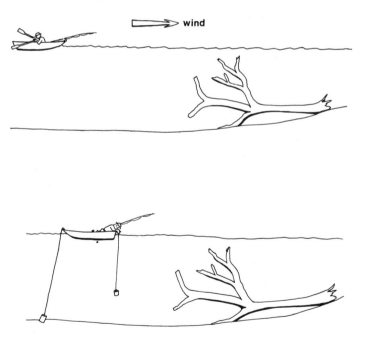

Fig. **O**

Most plugs, of course, do not have weed guards on them, nor are they easy to construct on plugs, so recourse to weed-guarded *spoons* is necessary if the angler wishes to fish *in* the tree.

This outlines one way of working the plugs from a boat. Broadly speaking there are two other ways: casting from a slowly drifting boat, perhaps assisted by the use of drogues or an otter board, and trolling. The former can be carried out under any conditions, a drogue slowing down the movement under strong winds and drift, but is most pleasant under relatively calm water conditions. Fish can be approached very quietly, but perhaps there is a tendency to cover the area too rapidly.

For many years one was advised to sit down in the boat during casting, but our own experience is exactly the opposite: good accurate casts, long casts, and proper working of the lures can only be achieved in the standing position (as shown in Photo 45). Obviously, great care must be exercised, and it is advisable (whether standing or sitting) to wear a life-jacket. Life-jackets are not designed with anglers in mind; they make casting a little awkward at times, and there is a great temptation to remove them. Don't.

45 Casting from the standing position.

When trolling plugs it is a help if two rods can be used as shown in Fig. P. The rods should be firmly held at the butt, and the best boats have a bar of wood for this purpose. Personally we feel that a couple of soft pads on the stern should be used to take the mid-section of the rod. This prevents damage to both rod and line. The anti-reverse mechanism should be *on*, since there is little point in having the handles spin round when a fish takes, or indeed in having the slipping clutch set very light. The fish may hook itself in its strike, but even so the angler needs to be pretty quick to the rods. Clearly, heavier line is needed for trolling like this and we would advise something like 20 lb breaking strain for pike fishing, for example. When fishing the same swim 'on the drift' one could probably manage quite well with 12–15 lb line.

An improvement on the above system is to have one person rowing and the other watching the rods, even holding one of them. The main trouble with this method is that when a fish takes it is always *you* doing the rowing, never the other fellow! The echo sounder, mentioned later, is a boon whatever trolling system is being employed.

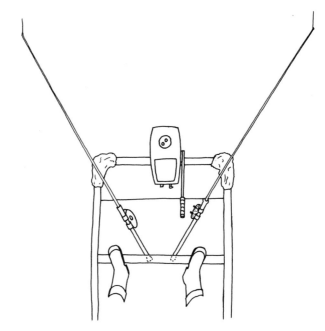

Fig. **P**

ELECTRIC MOTORS

There are few things better in this world than watching a fellow-angler rowing whilst you are fishing. There you sit, pretending to rig the tackle, whilst the other chap pulls the boat in ever-diminishing circles until finally you reach the place you didn't intend to fish. On a more serious note though, the boat with two in it is ideal. But there is a different situation entirely with the single-handed boat.

For a start you are rowing with your back to where you want to be looking, so in theory at least you are forever seeing where you should have been fishing; in practice you are acting the owl and trying to turn your head through 180 degrees. Nor is that all the problem, for having found the place you want to cover, you have then to ship oars, and in all probability turn round in the boat to face into the fishing area. And that, no matter how careful you are, means noise and disturbance.

So the answer is an outboard – not one of the petrol jobs. We were lent one of the Shakespeare Electric Motors to try, and immediately realised this was the answer for the single-handed angler. Nothing could be simpler than this piece of machinery. It is light, can be mounted on to the stern, and clipped to the 12-volt battery off the car for power. With a little sensible use there is at least five hours running which will still leave some life in the battery to start the car on the journey home.

The controls are simple enough – on and off. There are more sophisticated models available where the running speed, on/off controls etc. work from a foot pedal, leaving both hands free to fish. But we managed easily with the one lent us. Maximum speed is around three knots, and the whole engine is absolutely silent. No fuss, no mess, easy to start, and just a steady 'plod' to where you want to fish.

We didn't try it for trolling, but would imagine it would be useful in this capacity. We also discovered that if water conditions and wind pressure were bad then the engine could be turned through 180 degrees in its mounting, and the boat pulled instead of pushed – a better, more stable proposition where the bluff stern of the boat is made to meet the weather. One final good point – the price compares very favourably with the petrol alternative. In fact, one of these with an echo sounder and the plug man has just about every modern aid in the calendar.

46 Ray Webb setting up the Shakespeare electric motor.

What about landing fish? Gaffing is much easier from a boat than from the bank. In the first place one can get really close to the fish and more or less above it. For sea-fishing and salmon fishing when the fish is probably going to be eaten, a short-handled, round-bend gaff is ideal. For pike fishing the same, but with a V-shaped bend (Fig. N on page 92) for insertion under the tip of the jaw is ideal. Netting can be a problem if the net has a long handle; whilst the netting itself is a terrible nuisance if it is actually *in* the boat. It *always* gets tangled up with the plugs. Fortunately, Bill Keal came up with an ingenious system that we'd never heard of until 4–5 years ago. A triangular net is used, with the arms in the relaxed position, and it is hung over the side as shown in Fig. Q. Before netting it is lifted clear of the row-lock or pin, the arms held open, and the fish slid into it. At this point the arms are *closed* and the whole bundle lifted aboard. The same procedure can be used less efficiently with a rigid, round-framed net.

Fig. **Q**

Well, by now you are probably wondering what on earth to do with the hundreds of plugs you have, if the boat itself is full of all this para-phernalia. If we had a set of dream plugs (see page 26) and commo-dious pockets there would be no problems at all. As it is, one has to find a place for the plug boxes as well as the lures that are actually being used most often. The former should be placed under the seats if possible, and the latter can be thrown loosely into a Woolworth's toolbox (plastic) which is our usual system, or they can be hung on the gunwhale or on one of the strengthening struts (see Photo 47). Better still, we suppose, would be to design some kind of board upon which the plugs could hang, and which could be leant against the side of the boat.

All this sounds very complicated but in reality it isn't, and we would return to our theme at the beginning that plug fishing from a boat, particularly in clement weather, is a most delightful pastime. It is pleasant to cast plugs and watch them work right up to the boat, perhaps coming up from depth with a rampant pike in full pursuit,

47 A simple lay-out of plugs, all within easy reach of the angler.

and it is equally pleasant to get a good fish or two this way. Some would say more than pleasant.

ECHO SOUNDERS

One of the most important requirements of the would-be plug enthusiast is an accurate knowledge of the depth of the water, not just where he happens to be fishing at the time but over as much of the water as possible, so that he knows where the ridges, ledges and deeps are in relation to his casts. We spent many years plumbing waters by the laborious, though not unenjoyable principle of casting out a sliding float above a lead weight that would sink it. Several casts had to be made in each place, carefully adjusting the stop-knot for the sliding float between casts. It took a long time to obtain even a *rough* idea of the bottom contours.

48 Echo sounding. Graham Haylock with his inflatable boat preparing for a survey.

To give you an example of the advantages of an echo sounder, we have just contoured in detail a river and lake complex in two hours, using a small boat and Seafarer Mk II sounder. Plumbing the depth from the same boat, using a line marked in feet, would have taken at least a full day's work and the picture obtained would have been approximate to say the least. From the bank, only a rough and incomplete picture could be built up, and that would have taken more than two days' work.

Of course, the plug fisherman has another rough and ready technique he can use on a swim-to-swim basis, namely, that of using a diving plug and retrieving it until it hits the bottom. By varying the length of the cast, and then the angle of the cast to the bank, an idea can be obtained of the variation in bottom conditions, position of weeds, sunken trees and other obstacles. It is a time-consuming method, extremely costly in terms of lost baits, and a most skilful way of finding snags!

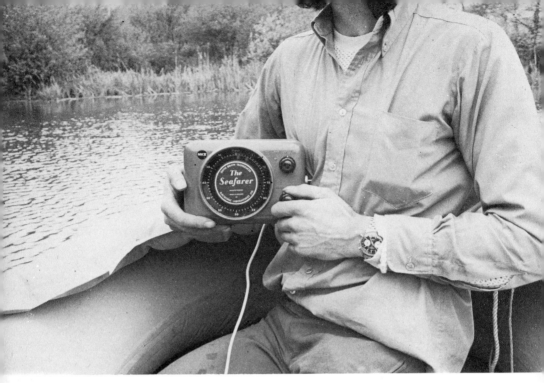

49 A close-up of the Seafarer Echo Sounder.

Therefore, whether one intends bank fishing a water or not, a more or less complete picture built up from echo soundings is an enormous help. We've mentioned the Seafarer Mk II simply because this is the excellent tool we happen to have used. At today's prices the cost is less than £40, but even so needs the funds of several anglers to make it a really worthwhile investment. We borrow ours from Eric Hodgson, the northern specimen hunter!

The machine is quite easy to use and consists basically of two parts; the main body which holds the battery and a dial on the front, and the transducer which hangs over the side of the boat. We usually place the body of the sounder on a piece of sacking in the bottom of the boat – in a safe position where nobody will kick it over or tread on it. The transducer is the particularly sensitive part of the equipment and under no circumstances should it be dropped or knocked. We attach ours as shown in Fig. R, tied to a lath of wood which protects the head of the transducer. But it can also be inserted in a piece of polythene tube as shown in Fig. S. The main thing to remember is not to row into the shore in such a manner that the transducer knocks on rocks, logs, or the bottom generally. Always unclamp it as you come in to land.

The manufacturers of our particular echo sounder include instructions on how to read the dial, which we have summarised in
Fig. T. For plug fishing set the switch to 'feet', since it is unlikely, if
not impossible, that you will be operating at depths over 60 feet.
There is a fathom setting for deeper water, but even those anglers
using plugs at sea are unlikely to be fishing at great depths.

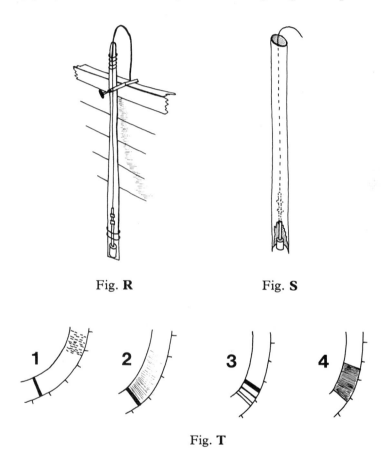

Fig. **R**   Fig. **S**

Fig. **T**

When over a hard, level bottom such as clean gravel, the neon
indicator shows on the dial as a clean hard line (Fig. T1): a sensitivity
switch allows one to 'focus' the echo. If a hard bottom is covered by
a layer of mud then this shows as a layer of fuzziness on the *shallow*
side of the hard line (Fig. T2). Thus the hard line may register at 20
feet, and if two feet of soft mud overlay the gravel then the neon will

show a fuzzy mark between 20 and 18 feet. Similarly, five feet of weed growth would show as fuzziness or intermittent flashes between 20 feet and 15 feet. Shoals of perch, bream etc. will show up quite clearly, but in our experience the thinner branches of a sunken tree have a similar effect on the reading: in either case the position of the bottom and of the shoal or snag shows clearly.

Irregular rocky bottoms usually have a hard line approximating to the upper level of the rocks, with intermittent weaker flashes *below* it (Fig. T3). Slopes which are particularly steep show as a broad but clear band (Fig. T4). Some idea of the usefulness of the equipment can be gained from the fact that we recently discovered a steel hawser stretched underwater between two islands: naturally, it had claimed its share of tackle and lost fish.

The plug angler afloat is placed, therefore, in a quite enviable position in that he can anchor his boat in a position adjacent to a good shelf, weed bed, or sunken tree and work his lures around them; or he can pick a good line along which to troll (or trail) his plugs. In the last case, naturally, he can keep the echo sounder working so that he can 'follow the contour'. Since he will know the depth at which his plug is fishing, you can see that this is an extremely positive approach to trolling. After an unproductive run along a particular ledge with the lure, say, three feet off the bottom, a second run can be made with the lure at a different depth. The important point is that the angler has a really good idea of the depth at which his plug is working, and of the nature of the bottom below the bait.

Following the contour is not a very easy matter in some cases where great variations in depth take place, but in large lochs and rivers it is quite possible if reconnaissance mapping has been carried out beforehand. Even on small variable-contoured lakes short, accurate trolls can be carried out, although here the angler will probably revert to the 'anchor-and-cast' system.

13

Clothing

There is only one thing worse than being wet when you are fishing – and that is being cold. If you think of all the work that goes into making a day's sport – the preparation, planning, expense of extra tackle, and then consider the sheer misery of being totally unprepared for the weather, you quickly realise that putting on a coat and rushing out of the house can be a criminal waste of time.

There is another side of the coin that is also frequently overlooked. When you are cold then both physically and mentally your power of concentration and reactions are impaired, a fact that our American cousins are well aware of, as any reader of *Field and Stream* during the winter months' issues quickly gathers.

It is not suggested that one should prepare for the Arctic, but few will dispute that better plug fishing is sometimes enjoyed during the cold months, so a little thought on the question of clothing is well spent. These pages so far have concentrated on minimising weight, and this is equally important in this sphere. Several thin layers of clothing that trap air between each item are better than one thick heavy coat. Mobility, allowing blood to circulate, is equally important.

Perhaps that is why we feel those one-piece suits, ideal though they may be for the specimen-hunter who camps on the bank, are unsuited for plug fishing. The gap of 'separates', i.e. jacket and trousers, allows much greater movement. A string vest, one or two woollen sweaters, and a Barbour-type coat will be found proof for the majority of English winters. Thigh waders over thick trousers, or Wellingtons with waterproof trousers (preferably a little on the baggy side) take care of the lower regions. Incidentally, the trouser legs fit *over* the Wellingtons, and not into them. We can cite at least one famous (?) angler who always wondered why he got wet feet when he fished in the rain.

But it is the 'etceteras' that are really important. As an instance we glibly mentioned waders. Thigh waders must be at least one or two sizes too big to allow for either woollen oversocks or Husky-type bootees – plus enough room for the toes to wriggle around and keep the circulation on the move. Equally important is the necessity to hang waders up by the feet so that air can circulate through them and dry perspiration etc. before the next outing. Of course, the same applies to Wellingtons, except that when it comes to drying the latter they are better filled with bran (used later for roach fishing) or screwed-up dry newspaper.

At the other extremity we are both agreed that when headgear has to be worn then there is nothing to beat a hood for keeping out wind and rain. Those tweed fore-and-aft deerstalkers, and poncey pork-pie titfers are ideal for bar-room boasting and emergency boat-sickness, but useless for keeping rain out of the back of your neck. Mention of the neck reveals a weak chink in the angler's garb, one which Ken learned to cure in the navy by the simple expedient of rolling a large soft hand-towel and using it as a scarf. It keeps all the draughts out as well, and when wet, only requires refolding to present a dry portion to the skin.

Hands are perhaps the most difficult of the extremities to warm, and gloves as such are obviously useless. Millarmitts are ideal, warm and possessed of long wrist pieces that tuck well up into the coat sleeves. Two pairs are better than one, so that a change can be made when it is really raining hard, and half the morning has been spent clearing weed from the trebles of the plug. Slightly more expensive are the shooting mitts made of leather by the same firm, but they are completely finger-free, only the hand and backs of the fingers being covered. They possess the extra virtue of being more hook-repellent than their cheaper woollen counterparts. Hand-warmers are worth carrying and when fingers go too blue to feel, then five minutes with one in each hand works wonders. They tuck into the inside pockets when not in the hands, still giving warmth to the body.

Fishing in the orthodox style provides a means for an angler to sit, either on box or stool. When plug fishing one is forever roaming, and a seat of any sort is an encumbrance. But sit one must, and this is when it is possible to collect the supreme accolade of the wet backside, worn for the remainder of the day in extreme discomfort. One sure and simple way to avoid it is by folding and tucking a large plastic bag into an inside pocket. It can be produced to sit on in seconds, and serves a dual purpose as a fish carrier if one turns up for the pot.

Warmth and concentration do not only centre on clothing. Food and drink are equally important. Each to his own when it comes to the likes, but we tend to avoid hot curries, Oxo or Bovril in a Thermos, all of which tend to leave one with a severe thirst. Scotch, rum and other spirits are warming for a time, but rapidly produce a chilling effect as the 'glow' wears off. A half-pint of tea or coffee in a Thermos, with sugar and dried milk carried separately, occupies little space and genuinely warms, especially if the contents are generously sweetened.

We mentioned the American scene in the early part of this section, and the severe weather they encounter during winter. It is very easy to scoff, and say that England provides nothing like that – but each individual feels the cold in different ways. Hypothermia – cooling of the body – is silent, insidious, and can be lethal. It is so easy to play the 'he-man', and carry on even if you feel chilled to the

50 Annual outing of the Old Plugonians Club. Martin Gay, Barrie Rickards, Ken Whitehead and Ray Webb preparing to lose some tackle.

very marrow. Nature gave us an in-built warning of this situation, the simple act of shivering. When it starts, run round, eat, drink, and in most cases it will stop because the body has warmed. But if despite everything that you do, the shivers continue, then is the time to head for home, or at least shelter and warmth. There is nothing great about collapsing from the cold miles from anywhere, and in-conveniencing others who have to look for you. Think and plan for the cold, and immediately your fishing will improve.

14

History of tackle

The history of plug fishing tackle is completely tied to the development of the reel. We fish today and never think of yesterday, and the tremendous problems of getting a bait out from the bank. In those early days it was very much a case of Hobson's choice, and there was nothing unusual in watching an angler strip yards of line off his reel to hang in coils at his feet. The coils were then reversed – and the line (in theory) flew sweetly through the rings as the cast was made.

In practice, every bit of gunge and grot on the bank got caught in the coils, or the line caught round the angler's clothing and after travelling about 15 feet the whole thing came to a sudden stop, leaving the angler with a Natural Disaster Area on his hands. Of course, there were the clever people who could cast directly from the Nottingham reel; an art of flipping the reel just before the cast was made, supposedly giving the reel initial movement to cure possible overruns. But the 'reel' problem lay in stopping the line gently at the end of the cast.

The progression from this was the Silex reel that had a few knobs and dials which applied both drag and brake. Actually, many anglers still found this difficult to master, and there are Silex models in existence that have the outer edge of the back plate cut away so that thumb pressure could be applied to the rim of the drum as a brake.

It was the 1930 era that produced the cream of centre-pin reels. Allcock's magnificent Arial reel could, and did, cast well straight from the drum, and they are in demand as working items and collector's models today. In fact many anglers swear that nothing has ever been made to surpass it. Of course, the Malloch reel mentioned earlier in the book was also in vogue, but it took a chap by the name of Illingworth to come up with the answer to long-distance casting, and the mass production of fixed spool reels has advanced to this day.

Quite how the multiplier evolved is lost to both of us. But we do know that the Elarex, made by Hardys, was the leader in the field and continued to be for years. Although no longer made, there are hundreds of models still giving yeoman service along the banks to-day.

Rods in the history of plug fishing? Well, earlier we said there was nothing new under the sun, and this is certainly true of rod design. Ken has a magnificent 6-foot split cane steel-centred Hardy Victor spinning rod. This dates from about 1910, and was known as the Overhead Victor, being intended for single-handed use, and supplied with a red rubber-covered handle below the winch fittings. The rod was intended to be matched with a small Silex reel, and balanced beautifully for accurate single-handed work. There were numerous small accurate rods produced through the pre-Second World War years, all of which contributed to the plug caster that we know today, and in these earlier stages were always of split cane. But with the war and its aftermath appeared metal. Phluger's were producing a stepped 6-foot caster around 1942, and Accles and Pollock produced several excellent casting rods in this country on the same lines in the 1947 era.

From here the glass-fibre rod that we know hit the market in just about every shape and form available – good, bad and indifferent! But the scene must change and carbon-fibre has yet to really reach us, with a whole new range of actions. It is for the angler to translate that action into plug attraction – and fish.

Electric reels have existed for some years, and so have electric plugs, with eyes that light up, and vanes that work from a small motor. You laugh? Well, they are in use on the other side of the Atlantic, and there is a shocking tendency for American yesterdays to become our tomorrows. Wait until they develop the pocket plug selection computer!

PART THREE

Plug fishing

15

Plugs and pike

It is not possible to learn *everything* about the pike and its activities by just going plug fishing all the time: but it is possible to learn more of them at this branch of the sport than at any other. Of the many thousands of anglers live- and deadbaiting for pike, including ourselves we would add, few have seen a pike take the bait. But in plug fishing and, indeed, in spinning, even a poor angler can observe the take of a pike quite frequently – always assuming that the angler is not so poor that he gets no takes! You get a terrific idea, for example, of the pike's vision in clear water. When Barrie used to fish Saltmarshe Lake in the East Riding with a small, yellow, plastic floater the pike seemed to see it clearly from at least ten yards away and they came at it like arrows. It was no good waiting for the bow-wave of the charging pike to reach the lure: the pike was always some feet ahead of the bow-wave, rather like the way in which the boil of water is some distance away from the rock which causes it in a trout stream. You can imagine the tension before the strike. There you are, craftily working a 4-inch shallow-diving floater over the tops of semi-submerged soft weed beds, when you see a bow-wave start off at ten to fifteen yards away as the pike homes in over the top of the same weed beds. If it's a small pike it will be only a foot or so ahead of the ripple, but if it is a big one it will be at least five feet in advance of the wave. Everything happens so fast that you get just about enough time to take a firm grip on the rod with one hand, and the reel handle with the other. Too often the pike slows down just before the impact you hope for, and follows the plug to the bank. It is at this point that you get a good view as it slides along. It may be a tiddler or a giant – and will it take just as you lift out the lure? On Carlton Towers Barrie once had a pike come out of the water and take the lure as it hung three inches above the surface.

When a pike follows the plug right to the bankside it often *does* take just as it thinks the prey is escaping. If it sees you, however, it either stops and sidles away slowly, looking agitated, or else it departs with tremendous acceleration and you are left with your plug swirling in the boil of water the pike leaves behind. Thirty yards away you see the bow wave subside, and then you lift the plug from the water for the next cast knowing that in all probability you frightened *one* pike for an hour or two. It is impossible not to be impressed by the take-off of a pike from a standing start, and it is this power that overhauls the prey, unlike the wearing down tactics used by perch and zander as they worry away at the tail of their prey.

Of course, this kind of excitement is best enjoyed in shallow, clear, weedy waters. In deeper waters the pike often appears from nowhere, gives you a terrific shock as it strikes, and has much of the advantage of any surprise attack, at least in the early stages of the battle: they often tear the reel handle out of your hand because you had lost concentration and held it lightly. At this point, with the rod flapping loose as it were, you often fail to set the hooks and lose the fish anyway.

The actual takes vary tremendously. Occasionally they *do* give the pluck-pluck type of take typical of perch, but more commonly they engulf the rear end of the plug and give the rod a tidy thump which is difficult to miss. Sometimes there seems to be real ferocity in the attack, particularly it seems to us, if it has had to chase the plug across the weeds, or hit it before the plug leaves the pike's hole in the weeds. We've never been certain, because things happen so quickly, whether the pike comes at the lure with its mouth agape (a phrase beloved of many writers) or whether the gaping mouth and flaring gill-rakers are the pike's quicksilver responses to its realisation that something is wrong. We're inclined to think that the latter is the case, and that on the strike it only opens its mouth at the last split second, and then only the bare minimum necessary to grab the plug. If the attack is fast and violent, with little time to think on the part of the pike, it probably hooks itself, realises its mistake and *then* opens its mouth wide and shakes its head. The angler's reaction is invariably a little slower and he probably *sees* the pike for the first time at the mouth-opening stage of the strike. Looked at like this the angler's strike is probably superfluous, except that it helps to knock the pike off an even keel at a very critical stage of the battle.

Another kind of take often ignored by the inexperienced is the slack-line bite. This happens when a pike follows a lure and hits it from behind but doesn't stop as it reaches the lure. The line goes slack as the pike continues its run. Any angler who has used a Veltic or Mepps spinner will know the feeling because these spinners 'go slack' if they pick up a little weed, and the best response is to reel faster until you catch up again. It's the same with a slack-line take on plug, except that we can't resist striking hard the moment things go slack! If you treat slack-line bites in this way, then the strike has to be sweeping enough to take up the slack *and* drive home the hooks, and remember you do not know how slack is slack. . . .

The kind of situation when the pike follows the plug right to the bank is the most difficult one for the pike angler to live with. What should he do? Reel faster; slow down; stop? If the pike has not seen you and the plug is not too close to the rod tip then all you can do is stop reeling and hope. With some plugs the pike will take them as they stop and float to the surface. If the plug is a sinker they may follow it down and take it. We find, on the other hand, that merely slow-

51 Well-hooked, but the misshapen mouth suggests earlier hook damage.

ing down a retrieve rarely seems to result in a positive take.

There are other ways of tackling this particular situation. Let's look at the whole problem of bringing the plug close to the bank. One difficulty is that the pike may see you; get round this by using every inch of bankside cover. On the Old Bedford River in the Fens there is little cover and the banks are very quakey, sending vibrations along ahead of the angler, so that it is necessary either to stand well back from the water with the merest inch of the rod tip sticking over the water, or to kneel behind what cover there is. Another trick is to use a longish rod, say ten feet or so, and bring in the plug to a position ten feet down the bank from where you are standing, rather than sticking the rod straight out over the water in front of you. One obvious disadvantage with short rods is that you *have* to bring in the lure to your feet.

There are many other things to be learnt from plug fishing in shallow waters than watching and getting used to the take. You learn the kind of lairs that small and big pike prefer, and you get an inkling of the presence of groups of pike in one place – hotspots – though the real recognition of these phenomena comes more easily through dead- and livebait fishing. On the other hand, a first-class plug fisherman can detect hotspots a little more quickly than a bait fisherman since the latter's techniques are necessarily a little slower. Barrie well remembers Basil Chilvers working his plugs along a Fenland drain and pinpointing a short stretch that he suggested we move into with baits. Since it was the depth of winter at the time, we expected – and found – that baits were rather better than plugs.

TIME OF YEAR

Time of year is an important consideration for the plug fisherman. Generally speaking the summer months are best for plug fishing for pike. In Eire, where there is no close season, coarse fish plugs, like natural baits, seem to succeed best in May, give or take a little. In Britain the months of June and early July are good, late July and August usually poorer, as indeed they are for all aspects of piking; and then sport picks up again in September. How long into the winter one can keep on plug fishing with a real hope of often beating natural baits probably depends on the year in question: a good year will provide lively fishing until well into November. But when the water gets cold, say around 47° F or less, then sport falls off rapidly.

Naturally we are generalising above, and there are enough exceptions to keep the ardent plug fisherman going right through the winter. There is also a number of waters in every region which respond well to plug even in the depths of winter, and not necessarily to small pike only. Find those waters and you have an added string to your bow if you are a general pike fisherman as well as a plug enthusiast.

It is worth remembering that as well as the pike getting cold in winter, so does the angler. You will often read how plug fishing keeps you warm in winter: much warmer than sitting down watching a deadbait. It doesn't. It has now become accepted in other fields of sport that to keep warm it is necessary to keep a thin layer of warm air next to your skin, between the clothing and your skin in fact. All that activity does is to squeeze this layer of air away, and constantly replace it with cooler air which the body then has to warm up. To keep warm this way you'd have to be stoking up constantly with food! So wrap up well for winter plugging, preferably with thin waterproof gloves as well, for it is constantly necessary to remove wet weed from the treble hooks.

Of course, temperature problems are not confined to the winter. In summer, during the occasional bouts of hot weather which we get, to carry plug box, net or gaff, and clothes through brambly undergrowth, from swim to swim, is a killer. Summer plugging is best enjoyed in the early morning or late in the evening, but it may well be that the best time for pike is just before lunch.

PLUGS VERSUS SPINNERS

We'll begin here with a generalisation. We have known few occasions when a spinner has been taken by a dour pike in preference to a plug, but have many times observed the opposite. Barrie first came across a clear instance of this many years ago whilst fishing a tiny pond near Snaith in the West Riding of Yorkshire. A perch he was reeling in was attacked by a good pike, but after a few minutes the pike fell off, as they are wont to do! He gave it a few minutes to come unscared, then cast a variety of spinners at it: it showed interest, obviously hadn't seen him, but didn't really want to know. The first cast with a small jointed wooden floater produced a great take and a fine pike of over 10 lb.

Similarly, in Ireland, he had a fish of 9 lb follow a worm to the boat, refuse spinner after spinner, and then take a plug first cast. That fish solved the problem of lack of a large landing net by leaping into the boat. It might almost have said, 'Unhook me quickly and put me back.' Which he promptly did.

On another occasion, also on an Irish lough, a friend spotted a huge pike sunning itself on the shallows. He cast various spinners across its bows and, even though it hadn't been scared off, it showed no real interest. But the moment a plug tried to wriggle past, the pike took it in a flash. That fish went over 20 lb. The many similar cases far outnumber the few occasions when a spinner or spoon has seemed to be better. On these rare occasions we have noticed that the pike will fall to a tiny twinkling spinner or spoon, such as a 1-inch minnow or a mackerel spinner, when they have been disturbed, or scared, or otherwise worked up by the use of big plugs. We'd certainly never be without a selection of spinners and spoons, as a back up to plugs which we prefer most of the time.

THE COMPLETE (TRAVELLING) PLUG FISHERMAN

One of the joys of plugging is that you stuff most of the gear in your pocket and gradually roam over a whole water, trying a swim here, a swim there. As we explained in the section on the dream plug (page 26) the question of a bulky plug box wouldn't arise if we could carry the bodies loose in our pockets and the treble hooks in a small box, but as it is one has to carry some kind of plug holder. If you cannot find a plug box with a carrying strap, then make a strap for one of the cheaper boxes. Better still, design your own carrying box to suit your own needs. Bill Keal, well-known pike fisherman for many years, used to dream of a really good plug fisherman's waistcoat with lots of pockets and attachment points for plugs. The scope for individual inventiveness is tremendous. Anyway, you'll have to carry a load of plugs if you intend taking things anything like seriously. In addition you need either a net or a gaff. Elsewhere in this book we have explained the *logic* of a plug fisherman carrying a light gaff. If you are also of this mind then you have no real extra burden to add to the rod and plug container. Personally, we still lug a big net with us everywhere we go.

It is obvious that anything but a *very* casual approach to plug fishing is going to be fairly arduous, and that the idea of rambling slowly from swim to swim is something of a daydream. What about the rod? If it is 4- to 5-feet long it will be no burden. The trouble is that delightful though these little rods are for casting and firing a plug accurately into a hole in the weed, we find a long rod (10-feet) much better most of the time – and we fish in some pretty tight places, too, not just fenland drains and reservoirs! It is easy to cast, even in heavy undergrowth, with a long rod. All you have to do is poke the rod through the trees and swing the plug out pendulum fashion. Perhaps the only problem is the fisherman's strike: a hefty strike will almost certainly take a branch or two along as well! And hitting a branch in mid-strike is one of the best ways of losing fish by failing to set the hooks properly. We've done it on several occasions. The important thing, of course, is to work out where you are going to strike, just as you should work out where you are going to land the fish.

52 One method of carrying plugs too big to fit the box.

APPROACH TO A SWIM

It is very common to see anglers march boldly up to the swim, stand bolt upright, lash out the plug as far as they can and then retrieve at considerable speed. A few more random casts are made, and then the angler marches stolidly on to the next swim. Such anglers may catch pike on plugs but they'd catch a lot more if they didn't frighten the pike away first. Without question, the best way to tackle a new swim is to walk up quietly and stop well short of it: try a short cast into the few yards of water immediately in front of where the bottom fisherman normally sits. It is a fact that pike are often attracted to these swims simply because the roach angler has been attracting roach, and one of the deadliest ways of plug fishing is to work your way along a match length a few minutes after the matchmen have packed up and gone.

Try a few more casts like this, preferably using a relatively small plug which has less chance of scaring the pike, and then move cautiously up to the edge of the swim, making full use of any cover, before searching the whole area of the swim more thoroughly. It's a good idea to begin with short casts, particularly along the edges to your left and right. If you suspect a pike has plucked at or followed

53 What next? Graham Haylock planning his attack.

the lure, and nothing happens on the next cast, give that particular part of the swim a rest for a few minutes whilst you search the rest: then come back to it with a few more casts. By then there will be a good chance that the pike has made up its mind and has no intention of being frustrated again.

Gradually increase the lengths of your casts until you are satisfied you have given the area a good coverage. Then you'll have to think about trying a different plug: a darker-coloured one perhaps if the sun has come out. You can imagine that all this procedure takes time, particularly if you try several plugs. Now you move on to the next swim, and do the whole thing again. Most writers tell you to work the casts *systematically* through the swim, say a whole series of casts angled at 5°. Our thoughts are that if you adopt this approach, and bear in mind that you have all day to fish, plenty of swims to try, and lots of different plugs, then there is a risk of the whole business becoming boring. If takes are few and far between then plug fishing like this can be the most boring fishing there is.

Personally we usually stick to one plug for a considerable stretch of water, and really give it a good trial. We do not work systematically through a swim: we try to cast to where we think the pike is most likely to be. In some swims we may make a few dozen casts, yet in others not make more than a couple. We reckon about an hour is long enough to fish at one stretch, for otherwise you lose concentration, and probably fish too, by fishing badly or missing the strike as the pike rips the reel handles out of your hand. So you need to have a relaxed, but careful and quiet approach to each swim, and try to *think* where the pike might be lying.

SIZE OF PLUGS

One thing that the modern trend to plug fishing and its publicity has done is to make anglers use plugs that are often too large. We're as guilty as the next man at this, for there is great attraction in the vast quantities of big American plugs now available. But plugs in the 1-inch to 3-inch category shouldn't be ignored, and as already explained, their very non-scaring qualities makes them a good bet to *begin* work on a swim.

There is another side to this question, however, and that is that pike often seem to *prefer* a small plug. We suspect that on many occasions a giant, shiny plug is not only fish-scaring because of the size of its splash, but fish-scaring because it is too new-looking and its counterfeit properties too apparent to the pike that sidles after it. So we would urge you to make a habit of using the smaller sizes of plugs like the River Runt Spook range or similar types. Of course, one major attraction of big plugs is that they cast a long way, but this is largely true of plugs in general when compared to spinners or spoons.

Big plugs seem to us to succeed best in big, shallow, weedy waters. Imagine that your cast goes fifty yards, then it doesn't matter too much if you frighten pike for a radius of twenty yards around the splash, because you have another thirty yards of retrieve left. The pike will be in pockets in the weed and will only vaguely hear the splash somewhere in the lake, and the thing they see is a fish working briefly above their heads: so they up and follow it. In deeper waters a big splash is probably appreciated by the pike over a much greater distance, particularly if the surface is calm.

COLOURS OF PLUGS

The beginner, confronted with thousands of plugs of almost infinitely varied hues, might be forgiven for thinking that anyone prepared to talk about plug colour was a little light in the head. But there *are* certain basic colours and combinations of colours that have proved highly successful over the years. But before taking a somewhat rambling course through the world of plug colour let's briefly tackle one aspect of light behaviour in water that is ignored by most anglers with almost deliberate care. It is this: white light is broken down when passing through water, for a variety of reasons, and the result is that a deep-fished plug does not necessarily appear the same colour to the pike as it does to us at the surface. We ought to say immediately that it is possible that pike do not see colour in quite the same way as we do anyway, although it is inconceivable that they live only in a world of shades of grey. Light then is broken down into its constituent colours, and the light which penetrates deepest is the blue end of the spectrum. Therefore, at depth, a blue plug ought to show up more clearly than a plug of any other colour, which would in fact appear as a dark colour. Whether fluorescent blue would show up even more clearly we do not know.

We're not aware that in general blue plugs have proved more successful at depth, although in East Yorkshire Barrie did rather better with 5-inch jointed blue plugs fished deep than with any other plugs in his tackle box. So there is a possibility that in the future some kind of pattern will emerge relating plug colour to depth of water.

That said, we can go on to what we think is the most important factor about colour to be fully confirmed during the last decade, and that is that on bright sunlit days a dull plug usually succeeds best, and the opposite on dull days. This has been known for a long time, but thanks to the efforts of the modern breed of ardent plugmen what was little more than a strong feeling before has been shown to be a matter of great importance.

It has been said, in explanation of this fact, that the bright light enables a pike to get too good a view of the lure before it hits it, and it seems a reasonable enough idea at first sight. However, we would expect that under bright light a dull plug would be more easily inspected simply because the flash from the flanks of a bright plug would tend to *obscure* details and dazzle the pike. Perhaps it's dazzle they don't like!

You can see the problem that this question of colour raises: it's no good having three different sizes of one plug, but it begins to sound as though you need several different colours as well, and hence you'll need three tackle boxes! It isn't as bad as that, of course, but we'd never dream of going plug fishing without our full colour range of home-made wooden Hi-Los, for example. We have a basically white one with a red head for dawn and dusk fishing; a green one and a yellow one, both rather dull, that we use when the light is moderately strong (say average light of a winter's day), and a black one with flecks of silver and a silver belly for use during the middle of the day. On one day a couple of winters ago we took pike all day long, gradually changing from light-coloured Hi-Los to dark and back to light in the course of the day.

However, it is impossible to have a comprehensive selection of different types of plug with you, and at the same time have a full colour range of each type, so you compromise by having, say, a white and red Hi-Lo, a darker Rapala, and a very dull River Runt Spook. In other words you have enough colour variation in each basic plug type – floaters, shallow divers, sinkers etc. – to cover most needs.

What about the actual colours themselves? Well, plugs which are basically either red or green we have not found very effective. There are exceptions, such as our dull green Hi-Lo and red and white Crazy Crawler, but the best colours seem to us to incorporate yellow in them somewhere. We had terrific success for years with a 4-inch yellow plastic plug that looked for all the world like a small pike nipping through the water. We have no doubt at all that a red throat and conspicuous eyes enhance the effectiveness of most plugs, whilst stripes of various colours, including green, upon the background colour are very important. Gudebrod's perch-striped Sniper is an extremely effective lure once the bright light of midday is upon you: as opposed to the rather gaudy yellow one which succeeds best when the weather is dull.

Naturally there is immense scope for invention and the artistically inclined. You can make brown plugs with nice red spots on like trout: ours do not seem to be any more effective than other colours, and if pike accept them as trout then they must do so with a barely-concealed grin. Great fun can be had by taking pike on plugs of many different hues – jet black ones at night, white ones in the middle of the day – and it all adds interest to a very fascinating kind of fishing.

PLUGS FOR DIFFERENT CIRCUMSTANCES

It will be apparent from much of the content of this book that there are plugs for almost any circumstances: they'll do almost anything except fly, from bumping along the bottom to crawling along the surface, popping on a calm surface, standing on their heads, or fighting their way through big waves. If you have a look at our section on the classification of plugs (pages 7–15) you will find one to suit most circumstances, but there will come a general realisation that most plugs are floaters which dive to various depths: sinkers are less common and true poppers or crawlers perhaps less common still. But some imagination can be used here. For example, if you do not happen to have a surface crawler in your box at the time, you can use a buoyant floater and retrieve it *slowly* so that it doesn't dive! Similarly, lacking sinkers, you can weight a floating diver in the manner shown in Fig. M (page 72), and often portrayed in American magazines, and work it through deep water knowing that if you get snagged up you will lose, in all probability, only the lead. We used this system with a little success on the deeper stretches of the Great Ouse.

Perhaps it is worth enlarging on this a little. Suppose you cast directly across the river, allow the plug to sink and then work it directly to your feet, repeating this about three feet further downstream, you cannot help at least disturbing if not attracting, at least several pike in every hundred yards. Most big pike sit down there on the bottom and they have to show interest or get out of the way. Looked at like that our results were not as good as they should have been.

One of the developments in the field of spoons during recent years in this country has been the use of weed guards on the treble hooks. Now with plugs you would not normally think of putting weed guards on several treble hooks, largely because weed is normally picked up by the diving vane first. But if you intend casting into sunken trees with sizeable branches (Fig. O on page 104) then there is no reason at all why you should not have a plug or two complete with weed-guarded treble hooks. They'll not help the plug through soft weed, but they'll help through logs: the diving vane need not be protected.

Therefore, one of the few places it is difficult to fish a plug is in weed beds which would constantly foul the treble hooks. Here the plug man *has* to revert to weed-guarded spoons, which are reasonably effective. Pike are often found deep *in* the weed beds (though not in soft, clogging weed) and not just around the margins where it is easy, and necessary, to fish plugs. Otherwise, using our classification guide, it should be possible to fish a pikey plug on the surface, shallow or deep, small or large, and fast or slow.

SPEED AND DEPTH OF RETRIEVE

About the biggest mistake made by beginners spinning for pike is to fish too fast and too shallow. This is understandable, for to fish slow and deep can be expensive in terms of lost spinners. It would be a help, therefore, if beginners used plugs, because if not fished deep they can certainly be fished slowly, thereby increasing the chances of a take by 50 per cent. Bearing in mind that in many circumstances pike may, in our opinion, prefer plugs to spoons or spinners, it is obviously very much better for a beginner to use plugs. Before very long he will realise that he can fish them in deep water, and when he finally appreciates through his own experience that pike lie deep most of the time the worry about losing lures will be a thought in the past.

With plugs you can easily search a water from top to bottom, but in general it seems to us that plugs are more effective fished as deep as possible in deep water. In shallow lakes, say 3- to 5-feet, this is much less important and they can be effective at all depths.

The speed of retrieve is naturally much slower with plugs: you can really make them wriggle, dive, and jerk at enticingly slow speeds. But we well remember extensive discussions with Fred Wagstaffe in which he insisted that with big plugs in shallow water a fast retrieve cannot be too fast for the really big pike. He reckoned they could overhaul anything the angler could throw at them. Thinking carefully about our own experiences we think this is correct, although we do not have a long list of big pike on plugs to prove it.

In conclusion, therefore, try to fish plugs at their best working speeds, usually slow, but have a number that work well at high speeds and try them in the shallow swims.

TREBLE HOOKS

Treble hooks on plugs for pike have two functions, one to hook the pike, and the other to be an effective keel to make the plugs work well. On larger plugs these trebles are enormous and therefore make hook penetration much more difficult. But a more important problem, which prompts these remarks, is that very small pike will *often* take big plugs, and the trebles can be quite damaging to small mouths; far more so than any gaffs on the market. We would urge anglers to unhook small pike with great care, because they certainly cannot avoid taking them by using big plugs. We might add that this is the only worrying aspect of plug fishing for pike which is otherwise one of the pleasantest forms of fishing.

Since treble hooks on plugs are usually large they are quite strong and this, coupled with the fact that they *are* treble, means that it is unusual to have a hook straighten out on you. This is not the case with the occasional *double* hooks you see on plugs. We have never seen a good double hook on a plug.

54 Come and get me! Action from a Crazy Crawler that lives up to its name.

Hook points on plug trebles are mostly poor: quite blunt with a ridiculously rank barb. The barb can be filed down, and the points kept sharp with a stone, as we described earlier in the book.

16

Plugs and perch

There is no doubt that the following pages should have a black edging. The perch, alas, has declined over the past years to the point that capture of one in any size and by any method will be guaranteed to bring a string of fellow anglers round to have a look. What was once an everyday occurrence, and in many cases the first real fish that a young angler caught, is now a relative rarity.

So it must follow that much of this chapter is drawn from our past experience, although Barrie has access to lakes that hold a good head of perch, albeit of no great size.

Although they are not separate species, perch have always been divided mentally by anglers into lake and river fish – with most serious angling being directed at the still water, as opposed to the more widely dispersed fish in the rivers. Undoubtedly the cream of perching has been in the big reservoirs and gravel pits, especially the various groups around London. Big shoals of fish would cram around the water inlets, pretty uniform in weight and size, and if the angler hit a day when they were 'on', then sport could be fast and furious.

The areas occupied by perch lent themselves perfectly to plug fishing; large open stretches, weedless and deep. Using a large sinking plug – a double-weighted Hardy Jock Scott was favourite – one cast as far as possible, allowed the plug to sink, and both twitched the rod tip and worked a slow retrieve at the same time. When a fish took it was always with a decided bang, and the majority of fish were hooked well inside the mouth on the tail treble.

The main problem lay in getting the plug down to the deep water where the biggest specimens would be feeding. Time after time it

55 A tight corner. Barrie plugging for winter perch on a lake.

was seized by small ($\frac{1}{2}$ to $\frac{3}{4}$ lb) fish within the first ten to fifteen feet of sinking. Eventually we took to clipping a small lead on to the trace fifteen inches or so above the plug, and although in theory that should have ruined the action, to all intents and purposes it made not the slightest difference.

Of course, there were times when the perch were just not on feed, and could in fact be as finnicky as any roach. On those days, no matter how or with what one fished, there was a distinct nervousness when a fish did take, apparent by the gentle plucks and the swirls of fish turning away at the angler's feet, having followed the lure in to the bank. Often a gimmick could tip the scales in the fisherman's favour, and a lobworm hooked on to the tail treble and left to trail was one of the more rewarding ideas.

Turning over some old copies of *Field and Stream* the other day it was interesting to note that pork strips are one of the things used in America, and now we wonder whether these, mounted in the same way as our lobworms were, would perhaps pay better dividends: bacon strips certainly work well with chub and pike.

Pond and lake perch have very definite areas that they prefer to live in, apparently regardless of the time of years, or the temperature of the water. But they can be as temperamental as Paddy McGinty's goat when it comes to a taking depth. Surface thrashers can be tremendously successful in pike styles and colours, Barrie already having described some of his 'tearing' experiences with the Crazy Crawler.

During the winter we have had most success around the reed beds – in fact there are times when perch can be heard moving among the stems, rooting for food. This is when a good loud splash from a floating-diving plug can pull fish, and the conditions for which a popping plug was designed. Mr Thirteen, Tiger, Trouble Maker, Sinner Spinner – all, in every combination of size and colour, are worth a try.

Occasionally it has been worth the trouble of groundbaiting where good perch are known to exist – especially where they are rather thin over the water, and fruitless hours would be spent in 'chuck and chance' fishing. We have used this method successfully on one particular Lea Valley pit, where the perch run big, but are few in number; we have also had success with it on the Thames, where perch are 'at home' in the deep water of sweeping beds. The principle is simple; just groundbait with a fine cereal mix, and fish for roach or bream in the normal way. When the small fry start cartwheeling and skimming on the surface, take to the plug outfit (after removing all bottom fishing gear from the swim) and work the water systematically.

The reverse can be worked; in fact Gerry Savage, who has access to some superb perch fishing in Kent, uses the style with great success. Here the angler suspends a livebait to work out in the water, and then works the water over with a large plug around the suspended bait. Result? In many cases nothing scores on the plug, but down goes the livebait float. It would appear that the plug incites the feeding urge in the perch which then goes for the livebait, to the satisfaction of the angler.

Gravel pits can be a never-ending source of surprise in perch fishing. During the working when excavation takes place, large amounts of spoil – clay and earth – are tipped back into the water at irregular intervals, leaving a series of ridges and valleys across the bed. Occasionally a deeper hole remains – and one, perhaps two big perch take up residence in that small spot. The difficulty of course lies in getting

56 Working the reed-beds for perch – a favourite hold in winter.

a plug into just that one position where it can be presented properly to the fish, bearing in mind that there are usually no landmarks to establish an exact location.

We know of one position like this, where a Gudebrod Bump 'n Grind will do the trick, providing it hits an underwater obstruction during the retrieve, at a distance of about thirty feet from the bank. In nine cases out of ten you can work the lure back across the bottom without success – then, on the tenth time it hits the rock, log, or whatever it is that projects on the underwater ridge, and after scraping over it, it will sink into deep water and be immediately taken. A foot to the right or left, and the hole is missed. One fish is usually all that the angler catches, until the next time out, when another fish will have taken up residence.

All man-made fissures on river or canals are favourite perch haunts – locks, lock cuttings, weirs, bridges, bank reinforcements (the famous 'camp sheathing' of the Victorian era), to name just a few places. But time and again the plug angler just doesn't give himself

57 The moment of truth. Ray Webb weighing a plug-caught perch taken from the Ouse.

a chance to really get a fish. He merely appears on the scene, has a few chucks with whatever happens to be his 'in' lure of the day, and wanders off convinced that nothing is to be caught.

These areas often hold exceptionally deep water, and we cannot repeat too often our earlier advice about finding a taking depth. Start on the surface, then change to a shallow diving plug, and work through the range to the bump and grind models. Remember to count the plug down – five seconds perhaps for the first cast, six for the second and so forth – until you really are scraping the bottom. Lose tackle? Yes, of course you may. But if you are really set on getting one of the big perch it is the only way of going about things.

Surprisingly few anglers who want to catch perch ever use anything approaching even a fair-sized plug. The myth of the small glittering perch lure has been going for years, and we feel sure that this is one of the reasons why few big perch ever seem to fall to the plug man. A 9-inch perch can comfortably manage a 3-inch plug in its mouth and still give a fight, size for size, equal to any other fish that swims.

Think big for perch – study the plugs we have discussed for pike plugging, and work on those lines, within reason. Remember also that perch eat perch, and when it comes to colour, a perch finish is often the most successful.

17

Plugs and zander

Zander have been around on the continent for a long while, and their North American counterparts, the walleyes, likewise; but in Britain, although of restricted distribution since 1878 they have been widespread in East Anglia for only a few years. Hence they are not *settled*, and the techniques used in their capture nowadays will probably have to be modified in years to come. Zander were introduced into the Great Ouse Relief Channel in 1963 and they have spread incredibly throughout much of the system including the rivers Wissey, Lark, Little Ouse, and Cam and the drains such as the Old Bedford, Sixteen Foot and Delph, as well as numerous other waters. Many of these waters are now good zander fisheries, and it all happened in less than ten years from an original stock of 97 fish.

In this recent period of spreading, zander livebaits and deadbaits have accounted for far more fish than have plug baits or spinners. It may be that as the zander spread into a new water and concentrate so strongly on mopping up the new larder of available small fish they become preoccupied with the natural fish to such an extent that they ignore things which do not quite conform to the pattern of dead and live fish. Nevertheless, plugs do succeed well at times; and the contrast between European and North American zander and walleye is worth pursuing further. In the longer-established populations where the zander or walleye do not form such an irregular percentage of the total fish population, and where there is more of a fine balance between prey and predator, the latter may be more on the lookout for anything worth eating. In any event, many more Dutch zander are taken on plugs than in this country, and plugging is an essential part of the North American walleye hunters' repertoire.

Quite a number of magazines and catalogues list particular plugs as being exceptionally good with zander or walleye. Creek Chub specifically mention the Cahokie, Crazy-z-fish and Viper; Bomber Baits list the Midget Bomberette; Heddon's rate the River Runt Spook, Punkin Seed, Sonar and Punkin Spin as walleye plugs. On the other hand, one does detect a certain reticence on the part of the publishers of these catalogues: pike, perch, game fish, crappie and bass are mentioned much more commonly than zanders or walleyes. We did a survey of those admirable Abu annuals called *Tight Lines*. It was surprising that very few zander were listed amongst their exceptional fish, notable exceptions being, in 1968, a $14\frac{1}{2}$-pounder on a Hi-Lo and in 1972, a 13 lb 3 oz fish on an Abu Killer. In 1970 Abu rated their Killer as a 'must' for zander. But in their catalogues in general few plugs are listed as 'musts', and the 1974 version of *Tight Lines* lists only a spinner (Atom) with a specific link-up to zander.

It is of interest that Abu's Killer is not unlike Normark's Rapala and Creek Chub's Viper, also rated highly as zander plugs. These resemble long, slim, silvery fish, and similar plugs have succeeded on occasions in Britain. We would tentatively suggest that in our experience, and on present evidence, live- and deadbaits are more successful than plugs on most occasions. The great attraction of plug fishing for zander is that when these occasions arise great sport can be had and probably more fish hooked and landed than when fish baits are used. It may be that the zander, being a rather sluggish fish without the turn of speed of the pike, is simply not prepared to chase a moderately fast-moving plug. Or it may well be that zander spend more time scavenging on the bottom than do pike and perch. We know one lake, admittedly not crowded with zander, where despite intensive use of spinners and plugs, not a single zander has been caught on anything other than fish baits or lobworms.

The last water was a crystal-clear gravel pit, and it is a fact that a considerable number of plug-caught zander in this country were taken under muddy or slightly coloured conditions on the Great Ouse Relief Channel. The fish were located as a shoal or hunting pack and the plugs were worked slowly through them. The fish caught were mostly in the 2–3 lb range and almost all of them were caught by casting parallel to the bank where the zander were chasing fry.

Most of these zander fell to single plugs of the River Runt Spook type or small Rapalas, or to relatively small jointed plugs. Just as many fell to spoons as to plugs. There is one major difference between the Great Ouse Relief Channel on the one hand and many other fenland drains and the Dutch drains on the other, and that is that the G.O.R.C. is very wide (about 100 yards) and relatively deep (about 12-feet). On the narrower and shallower Dutch drains plugs have succeeded well with zander for years and we fully expect that in the Fens they will really come into their own in future years.

For the present we would suggest using plugs like the Viper, Whopper Stopper's Hellcat, Norman's Shiner-minnow, Normark's Rapalas, and Abu's Killer and Hi-Lo, preferably in the smaller sizes and preferably in silver. The best times for plug fishing in clear water conditions seem to be at dawn for the first hour and at dusk, just as in bait fishing. There is no doubt that the zander come on the feed at this time.

Night plugging has also been successful on some still waters. Naturally you have to know the water well both with respect to where you put the cast and also where you put your feet! It is a good idea when casting in the dark to have a swan shot just above the top swivel of the trace, otherwise it is easy to reel the swivel into the top ring of the rod. A slight improvement on the swan shot tip is to tie a Billy Lane stop-knot about four feet above the top swivel of the trace: on the retrieve you feel the stop-knot enter the top ring of the rod. You can even have two stop-knots, one at four feet from the swivel and another at ten. The effect of this is that when you feel or hear the first knot click through the top ring you have ten feet to retrieve, and since this is a very critical time on *any* cast you can really concentrate. A fish taking in the dark when you least expect it does your heart no good at all.

At one time Barrie did a great deal of night plugging and spinning for trout and would confirm that too many surprises in the dead of a dark night are no good for anyone's well-being. Three such takes, particularly if you are dreaming at the time, are enough to send you off home for a short rest. Trout and perch both give a little warning pluck, however, before the main pull, but with pike and zander this is not usually the case: they hit the lure and that's that. If you are taken by surprise it is an easy matter to miss.

Results on plugs during coloured water conditions on the Relief Channel have been better than under clear water conditions. We remember one youngster taking four nice zander in as many casts by working a small silvery plug along the edge of the water. Several

58 Fish of the future? A plug-caught zander.

other anglers have taken nice fish *between* the reed beds and the bank when the river has been in flood: in these conditions the water is not merely coloured but *dirty*, carrying rafts of rubbish and quantities of submerged debris. But the zander get close to the bank, behind the reeds, and despite the oxtail soup appearance of the water good fish can be taken on bright plugs.

Another way to take zander on this water is to use a deep-diving or sinking plug and work it close to the bottom, particularly over the last few yards of the retrieve. Quite a few zander sit at the break of slope down at about 11- to 12-feet and will follow a plug that creeps up the slope. If the plug snatches at the bottom, kicking up little puffs of mud, then so much the better. They'll also tackle a plummet or a paternoster lead retrieved in this way, as Barrie knows from his own experiences!

Even in coloured water conditions it seems that dawn and dusk are the best times, although one's chances during the day are far better if the water is not clear. One technique is to keep a careful watch on the water surface about ten yards out from the bank and cast to any strikes. Zander often strike at fish near the surface when there is a good chop on the water, but of course the strike may easily pass unnoticed. Best of all is to spot a pack and detect the direction in which they are moving. By adopting a quiet approach they can be followed for some distance.

We think that, in the future, plug fishing in the Fen drains in general will become easier: quite a lot of the shallower drains will respond to more varied types of plug and to more varied techniques. But we cannot see zander chasing plugs with the ferocity of a hunting pike. Having watched zander take a plug it must be said that they follow it almost leisurely before taking a firm hold. Like perch, they really take a good look at it first. Occasionally they may take a pluck-pluck at it but then usually come short in the end. Clearly, from what we have said, plug fishing for zander has a long way to go in this country and we suspect that this may be to some extent true for the continental fisheries.

18

Plugs and chub

Angling literature through the ages leaves the reader with a firm impression that the chub is a rather coarse character that spends his whole time looking for the slightest excuse to disappear; an easy-to-catch but difficult-to-approach fish that might turn up in a roach swim – providing he deigns to leave the shade of the willow trees on the opposite bank. Always it is the willow trees – and always they are on the opposite bank!

Charlie Landells was responsible for Ken's conversion to plug fishing for chub. One back end day he took him to the Upper Ouse in a shooting brake, the engine noise of which was nearly drowned by the slurping and slooshing of a few hundred large slugs in varying colours busy gorging themselves in a large drum of garden refuse. Using a near spinning-type rod Charlie mounted a slug on to a spliced hook, and proceeded to throw this into just about every place that no angler in his right mind would ever consider casting – and produced fish after fish.

Ken sat and watched, soon realising that the sexual habits of the slug, apropos home-breeding in the garage, did not appeal to him in the slightest, nor did the aura of slime that covered hands, rod handles, and sandwiches. From there it was an easy mental exertion to imagine a plug landing in the water instead of a slug, and yet another chub-plugger was born.

It would be no exaggeration to state that three-quarters of all coarse fishermen do not believe that a chub would look at a plug for one second, let alone would take it thinking it was natural food. Probably the reasoning against the acceptance of this idea is that chub take fright easily, and a plug splashing on to the water would provide

59 Charlie Landells slugging a few chub out of the Upper Ouse.

that fright, so Q.E.D., the plug fisherman must come home chub-less.

Quite the reverse is the actual case. Chub are probably the most inquisitive fish that swim, and a 'plop' of any sort, providing it is not that caused by a half-brick, can be guaranteed to bring them imme-diately to investigate. *But only if they have no reason to suppose that an angler was or could be responsible for that happening.*

If you are using a leger or float rig you are constantly performing mental calculations around the possible action of the bait once it is in that difficult corner where you feel the fish might be. With a plug one has only to fit the bait into the corner, and control can be dictated by the angler from the second it hits the water. No float or lead pre-ceding the bait hang-ups, or fruitless fishing with a bait that has come off during the cast.

Long-distance casting is the exception rather than the rule in chubbing. Accuracy, however, is all-important, and only the man who knows and uses his tackle can hope to get where the best chub lie. Light, single-handed sensitive rods, rather on the short side and balanced with a sensible fixed spool reel take a lot of beating. In fact this is one of those occasions where the closed-face reel comes into its own.

Add a shoulder bag or fishing waistcoat into which a selection of lures can be packed with a few sandwiches (see Photo 52 on page 129) – and the plugman is prepared. No long-distance heavyweight stuff – a light landing net and off you can go with as much or as little water to cover as you can manage.

60 Alan Vare plugging for chub on a tiny feeder of the Hertfordshire Stort.

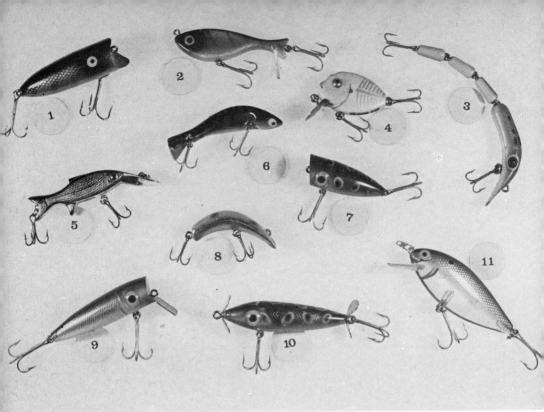

61 A SELECTION OF OUR FAVOURITE PLUGS FOR CHUB. They all appear in sections for other fish as well, but these are our 'musts'. 1. Mr Thirteen 2. Mr Murder 3. Beno 4. Punkin Seed 5. Snoky 6. Prowler 7. Trouble Maker 8. Lazy Ike 9. Basspin 10. Sinner Spinner. 11. Shad.

Perhaps a word on distance would not be out of place at this point. Take a long section of good chubbing river, and times without number the angler starts to flail the water and charge along the banks at a rate of knots. It is infectious – a touch of the water in the next swim being greener than that in the one you are fishing. But it is a forerunner of failure. To catch chub with a plug one must examine every possible hold, think like a chub, the chub that is possibly sitting there, and plan his downfall.

A preliminary reconnoitre is often useful on a strange water, an evening walk without tackle (if that is possible!) where the best parts can be earmarked for special attention. And of course, the more important detail – how to approach the possible fish without putting him down.

This is where the luxury of a boat can bring immense pleasure and reward, and where the electric motor comes into its own. Launch the boat upstream, drift down casting across under the banks on either side, or explore a small backwater, a weirpool, under the arches of a bridge; wonderful sport, the thing that angling memories are made from.

Where else do good fish lie? We talked about this one day at great length, and came to the conclusion that the large chub is a frustrated tortoise. He loves an armoured plating around and if possible below him.

So trees that overhang, roots that grow out into water, and sunken branches that have silted solid with bank and bottom make the obvious holds. Reed beds – especially thick rafts of reed mace and bullrush where it is possible to wade through long sections – rather like Amazon stuff – is great fishing, providing cover for the angler who moves quietly and allowing him to reach a hundred little channels and pools where the current has cleaned a passage. Bridges, and the pools that usually lie above and below them, landing stages, boathouse creeks off the main river and lock cuttings (especially where there is a reasonable current – the Kennet and Avon canal is an instance) also come immediately to mind.

Whilst thinking of man-made chub haunts there are few better places in which to enjoy sport than a weirpool. Part of this is a fascination for fast running water that acts as a magnet for a large majority of fishermen; you never know what might turn up! Quite apart from this, chub use the whole area as a natural feeding ground and lose a lot of their natural caution in so doing. Happy memories exist for Ken who has had great fishing on the Britford water, combing the whole weirpool for salmon and finishing with king-sized chub.

Kingsweir is another good weir chub haunt, where they lie just below the sill. Once hit, they double back under the rush of water and under the sill itself, which stands on stilts. Exciting and frustrating moments. Erosion and chub are well suited, and undercuts in the bank can usually produce a fish. Jack Hilton can read a water as few other men can, and to watch him size up one of his Norfolk rivers and point out the undercut sections – that are not always on the concave side of a bend – is an education in itself.

Having described the seemingly impossible places to fish we shall obviously be hammered by the critics if we don't give some idea of how to get a bait to them. Going back to our chub and tortoise comparison, it seems reasonable to suppose that where the tortoise sticks his head and tail out of the shell so, metaphorically speaking, the

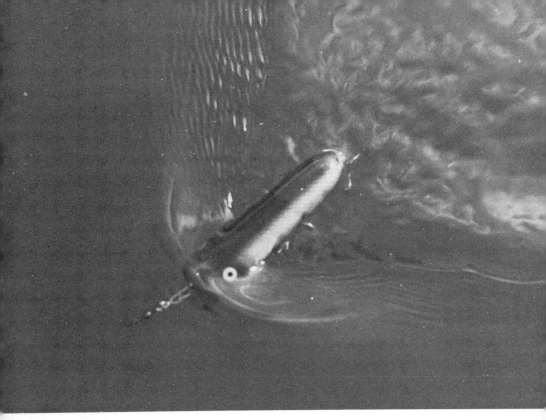

62 'Popping'. Note the two surface patterns caused by plug action when the rod tip is twitched.

chub must stick out one end for food, if for nothing else. Once that chink in the armour is found – exploit it.

It isn't necessary to cast directly into the chub all the time. Dapping, the time-honoured and oft-described action of poking a rod tip under or through the undergrowth along the bank, and then allowing the bait to drop on to the water, can be rewarding; it can also be frustrating and damaging to waders, trousers and dignity. Many plugs are designed to be 'twitched' and generally teased on the surface, and it is in these situations that they pay a dividend.

If the particular chub you want to reach is right at the back of heavily overhung trees, then don't try and cast to him. Select a floating plug, cast well upstream, allow plenty of slack line and leave the plug to drift down under the branches. Start the action when the plug reaches your fish – and you could be in business.

Underwater obstructions require a little imagination. It isn't always possible to see their full extent, so try probing. Use a shallow-

63 A plastic Otter, used to retrieve snagged tackle in running water.

or medium-running floating plug, and delicately 'feel' the plug back to you via the reel handle. The moment it hits an obstruction, stop reeling, drop the rod tip and in the majority of cases the plug will float up to the surface, free of the obstruction. The emphasis is on the word *feel*. Ham-handed reeling will only lose tackle. How does one tell the difference between the bump of an obstruction and the bump of a taking fish? Experience only, we fear – something that no amount of 'flannel' or 'bull' in writing will teach.

Lost plugs, especially at around a pound or two a time, is a worry that we feel puts many anglers off plug fishing. Our descriptions so far of how to handle tight corners has saved us a good few pounds – so has the angler's 'otter', a disc of plastic that can be slipped on to the line, fed down the water, and allowed by its shape to provide a side-strain above the lure. Photo 63 shows its use, and ours has been well worth its keep. But of course, they only work in running water, where current provides the lateral pull.

One of the most difficult places to fish without tackle loss is in and around weed beds of any sort. It is possible to tie weed guards on to hooks, but they are nowhere near wholly efficient. If a big chub is lying in the weeds and waving two tail-segments at you your only chance of making contact will be to look for a possible clearing near-by, land a plug right in it and fish as much of the open water as possible. When you reach the weeds, reel like mad and make an enormous strike so that the plug lifts from the water and (in theory at least) over the weeds. It is also not a bad idea to duck at the same time!

Now to the nitty-gritty – plugs themselves. By and large it is the small plug that brings the best possible results. Not that a chub cannot manage a big one – they don't call him satchel-mouth for nothing – but because it is action that counts where attraction is concerned, and a small plug is more versatile in this than its larger brethren, especially in confined spaces. How to describe them without making a book read like a tackle-dealer's catalogue is difficult, but we decided to 'zone' plugs into their main action heading earlier, so we shall take them in that order.

SURFACE LURES

Two Shakespeare models are first-rate surface lures for chubbing. The Slim Jim is a wooden torpedo with propellers at either end and fishes best on the 'try it and see' principle. You can guess what we mean by that – the sort of large hole that should hold a chub, and so you try the Slim Jim across the surface where it kicks up hell's delight. Usually the chub cannot resist having a look-see, and the rest should follow. This one definitely needs space though, otherwise the propellers can't really send out the message.

Mr Thirteen we have described elsewhere (page 24). The junior model measuring in at $2\frac{5}{8}$ inches and in the Yellow Coach Dog finish looks good, and fishes superbly. Another model more difficult to obtain in this country, but worth the effort of getting hold of, is the Lucky popper. This is an absolute natural among the lily pads with its 'popping' action.

The Bomber Stick and Spinstick models are similar to the Slim Jim in action, the Stick being rather unique in its fishing position of nearly vertical, and leaning slightly forward out of the water. We are in no doubt that noise from a lure across the surface can be a tremendous attraction, but we find extreme difficulty in convincing many anglers of this. The Arbogast Jitterbug is a good example of the noise attracters. The large down-turned shield at the nose of the plug sends twin jets of water spraying outward and at first sight would tend to put off even the most ardent fisherman. But times without number this lure has scored for us.

Heddon floating and diving plugs are first-rate, starting of course with the Meadow Mouse that is just about the most natural artificial

64 Sinner Spinner, showing the surface disturbance that revolving blades can produce.

65 The Meadow Mouse in action.

(pardon the pun) that we have ever seen. The Spooks, Wood Vamp, Vamp and River Runt have proved themselves time and again not only for chub, but every other type of coarse and game fish. Shakespeare's Dapper Dan, the Abu Hi-Lo, Rapala originals, and the Midge Oreno from Gladding's stable are also useful additions to the tackle box.

DEEP-DIVING AND SINKING LURES

These are more out of the tackle box in the winter months than during the summer, when weed has died back and it is possible to bump and grind (to quote the American jargon) along the river bed. They are also great in a weirpool during the summer months – providing you have guts. At about £1.25 or so a time, it certainly takes guts in every sense of the word to pull on a well-snagged plug. But the fish are there, and deep work in the deep holes that infest every weirpool can bring wonderful results.

Abu's Killer and Snoky, Bomber Baits' 200 and Punkfish, Shakespeare's Klatter Kat and Big 'S', Heddon's Deep 6, Spooks and Sonars give some ideas of our other fancies, and one that has reached us late but which bodes well, the Punkin Seed. It *looks* fishy, which we feel always instils confidence in the fisherman and is so necessary to bring results.

The Woolco range of plugs is worth investigating. They are very similar to many of the famous originals, but in a lot of instances are scaled down, and make ideal chub lures. They may need an odd touch with a file here and there to smooth out a rough casting, but price-wise they fit into the young or apprentice plug fisherman's pocket.

So far we have said little or nothing on the question of colour. There are two ways of looking at this; one is from the fishes' point of view, where one supposes that whatever is offered should look as life-like as possible, be it fish, insect or what-have-you. In this case the green, brown and predominantly yellow plugs would seem to be a must. Viewed from the angler's point of view, it is whatever takes his eye, and may result in some of the bright blues, reds, purples and orange colours that hit you when so many tackle box lids are raised. Perhaps this may be the root of the maxim that runs 'Plugs catch fishermen, not fish'. We would be the first to agree, however, that some of those with more garish decorations *do* produce fish, often when the more obvious natural doesn't arouse the slightest interest.

WEATHER AND WATER-TEMPERATURE

Obviously, so much must depend on the day. We were both brought up on the old spinning maxim that dull colours should be used on bright days and in clear waters, bright colours being the order when the water is dark and the light poor. Light has an enormous influence on fish, and strange though it may seem, the reverse is true of plug fishing for chub. When it is dull and overcast then get out the deep golds and blacks, keeping the light colours for the bright sunny days when the water is clear. Ken vividly recalls talking to an American

visitor in Pall Mall on the question of plug colour and light, and remembers his advice. 'Son', he said, 'when the water is not quite thick
enough to plough, and not quite thin enough to drink, and when
the camera needs an exposure of f5·6 with a fast film – that's the time
to go fishing.' Unfortunately he didn't say anything about shutter
speeds.

Floodwater is an exception that proves a rule, and when the banks
are nearly under water then the biggest, most agile plug in the box,
regardless of colour, should be worked through every inch of slack
water possible, and kept on or near to the bottom. Actually, the
fisherman is in double dilemma with these conditions. Using a floater
he can catch on surface debris and suffer a break; with a deep dive
or bump and grind he is pretty sure to catch on freshly exposed obstructions. But gamble one must.

Obviously, weather conditions are of great influence to any sport
and an understanding of them can only increase one's chance of a
fish – even be it only by making sure that you pick up the rod on a
taking day. But chub can be the most difficult fish to understand
where weather is concerned. Think about it. There it is, well down
to freezing, ice all over the banks and rushes bent down by its weight.
Lines of brass monkeys nipping down the towpath on their way to
get lagged when suddenly there comes a shout from a crowd of fishermen. Something has been caught – and in nine cases out of ten that
something is a chub. Now to the other extreme. Blinding heat that
brings practically all wild life except courting couples to a standstill, the river near-warm enough to boil an egg – and again, it is the
chub that allows his stomach to overrule his brain and so finishes up
on the bank.

Earlier, we mentioned the barometer and the fact that we believe
in its use. Obviously it cannot tell you when to fish or, better still
perhaps, when not. But two or three rules of thumb are well worth
remembering about its prophecies. A rapid rise foretells unsettled
weather, whilst a slow rise foretells the reverse. A slow, continued
rise over a period of time indicates to any sensible angler that it is
high time he told the office that grandma has just died, and to check
that the plug box is really full and ready. Our best days have been
those when the barometer has risen slowly in summer and the
weather has been 'soft', i.e. the light has been plentiful but not harsh,
and there has been a touch of moisture in the air – perhaps even light
rain – that has caused the temperature of the water to rise a little.

Obviously the better (higher) the water temperature, then the better are one's chances of sport, but there can be no hard and fast rule with this, e.g. our description of the chub, so often caught when nothing else moves. Again, Ken has often looked from his bedroom window on to the Lea, and seen that delightful and fascinating water-mist that comes when water temperature is higher than that of the air. In theory the perfect setting and conditions under which to catch fish; but time after time Ken has dropped everything and flailed the water without success.

Although the weather conditions can to some great extent influence sport, few anglers are going to let it influence them away from the water. It's just a question of trying that much harder when the cards seem stacked against success – and through all our talk of plug types, colour, size, the weather and the temperature, it is application that really matters.

Take each plug that you use and fish it as though it were the best in the world. Try to imagine what it will look like in the water from the fishes' point of view; run it back and forth at your feet until you are really sure of its action, then cast to the fish and get every ounce

66 Flood time. Adrian Lawson looking for slack water after the river has left its banks.

of teasing and attraction from it that is possible. Don't change it until you are sure that it has been presented to its best advantage – and then repeat the whole pattern with the next offering from the box.

Usually, a taking chub mouths the plug hard enough to be hooked without the need of a strike from the angler, especially when the lure is on the big side. It is when the smaller plugs are being used that a strike is necessary, just in case one of the small trebles hasn't found a hold inside that big mouth. But under no circumstances should this be the full-blooded swing that is associated with pike fishing. Although there is a large amount of hard bone and gristle around the mouth area, there is also a considerable amount of soft tissue from which the hook can easily be pulled, some of it on the outside, and a chub takes with such a rush that often he is hooked on the outside of the mouth, especially when the plug is being retrieved quickly.

Where one chub has been caught another will be found often within half-an-hour of taking the original fish. It would appear that on many rivers there is a housing shortage, and another fish of similar size to the first will take up residence as a vacancy occurs in a good lie. With this in mind, the effort of keeping a diary – even on very abbreviated lines – is well worth the effort, so that the known places where fish have been found in the past can receive regular attention.

19

Plugs and other fish

In these islands where plug fishing for pike and perch has always been popular, interest in recent years has received a fillip with the importing of North American techniques by anglers such as Fred Wagstaffe, and yet it is in need of much greater exploitation as far as other species are concerned. Plug fishing for salmon is a well-trodden path, and not really within our compass, so we shall say no more about it except that it merits a book on its own: relating taking colour and the lure size to the exact water spate conditions on different waters is almost an exact science to many salmon anglers. We have taken many hill-stream trout on small plugs, but on most trout waters today plug fishing is at least frowned upon, if not banned altogether. Not so in Ireland, where many of the big loughs are open to plug fishing. And the Irish trout provide a case of the required 'exploitation' that we have mentioned: on one large and famous lough the locals had for years used small spinners in the lea of the islands to take smallish trout in shallow water, and yet Wagstaffe and colleagues caught several trout over 10 lb in weight by braving the open lough and following the contours with an echo-sounder. They used plugs and other lures to find the taking depths, really stuck to their task, and eventually came up with a superb technique, the possibility of which had existed for years and yet had not been exploited.

Big sea-trout certainly take plugs well on some fenland waters, as do the fewer big brownies in with them, but the locations are well-guarded secrets. What interests us is that the plugs should be fished deep even when the sea-trout are leaping in numbers. At dusk and dawn a few will fall to a fast, shallow-fished silver plug, but mostly a deep and moderately fast retrieve is needed – faster than you would retrieve for pike and perch for example.

Very occasionally we read of other coarse fish being caught on plugs – bream, tench, carp, eels, and even roach. Most species are predatory to the extent that they will sometimes eat fish, particularly in spring and early summer when fry abound in the weedy shallows. Probably exploitation will be difficult. Bream will certainly take large lures, both spoons and plugs, but usually in spring and, in our experience, usually in Ireland! Even the bream of the Norfolk Broads do not seem to fall regularly to spinners during the Easter break in the close season.

What seems a real possibility is the construction of very small plugs, less than $1\frac{1}{2}$ inches in length, and fishing them on fine lines through shoals of roach, tench etc. in the early part of the season. Of course, very small plugs are already on the market, but it would be much easier and cheaper to make your own, particularly bearing in mind the probable loss of them to marauding pike. The smaller the plug is, the nearer it will approach some 'flies' in construction – the polystickle for example. We now know that these various trout flies or lures are highly successful with coarse fish, whether they are fished on standard fly tackle or on float-fished outfits, and there is little doubt that tiny plugs would succeed. The important thing may be to fish them through big shoals of surface-priming fish, since this is where we have best succeeded in Ireland.

The plug addict is not restricted to coarse and game fish, but can try his hand at sea-fishing for bass and pollack for example. We've had quite a few pollack on plugs as well as spinners, and mackerel will, of course, take anything that moves at times. Plug fishing for bass has become quite an art in recent decades and we do not wish to attempt a synopsis here, but rather to point in the direction of the ocean the angler who comes to plug fishing through his freshwater interests. Quite recently some well-known pike fishermen tried plug fishing for shark from a small open boat. Perhaps a little foolhardy, but the shark were willing to take the plugs so the sport has definite possibilities. You can even fish plugs much as you do perks or spinners, that is at depth, above a good-sized weight. We tried this years ago off Flamborough Head in Yorkshire and took codling on the plugs. Tangling the plug with the reel line was the main problem, but a little of the ingenuity for which sea anglers are well known would soon solve that problem: it is possible to fish the plug on a boom, just to mention one way around the problem.

Anyway, since there is a modern breed of angler who is not so much a fisherman, but more a plug addict, he should know that there is more to plug fishing than plugs and pike.